Praise for *Cow Hug T[...]*

T0037950

"*Cow Hug Therapy* by Ellie Laks should come with [...]
read this book, you will be transported into our original childlike wonder of the
world where we hoped to wake up with a circle of cows around us, meditating and
accepting us for all that we are. While reading this book, you'll shed tears that are a
beautiful and necessary jumble of joy, sadness, and awakening. Ellie's stories read
like a mix of a modern-day mystical-barnyard Beatrix Potter and James Herriot's *All
Creatures Great and Small*. The characterizations of these individual bigger-than-life
cows are true to form. I know because I've been fortunate enough to have a friendship
with Ellie and Karma. Every story is a delight, and the chapters progress through each
of the cows who shaped Ellie and the evolution of the Gentle Barn. I so wish I had met
Buddha, the cow who accidentally started Cow Hug Therapy."

— **Joan Ranquet**, animal communicator, author, TEDx speaker,
and founder of Communication with All Life University

"Our society is slowly waking up to the plight of animals, and more and more are
taking steps to help wherever they can. We are acknowledging that animals have feelings, wants, and needs, much like our own, and animals are now much more like
family members than ever before. But animals are also our healers, teachers, and
witnesses. This is illustrated beautifully in Ellie Laks's book *Cow Hug Therapy*, in
which she shares stories of some of her wisest and most resilient rescued animals at
the Gentle Barn and relays their messages of hope."

— **Montel Williams**

"Ellie Laks's experiences show readers that, contrary to traditional assumptions, the
benefits of the human-animal bond extend to species beyond our domesticated
pet dogs and cats. Relationships with cattle, horses, pigs, etc., are one of the most
underutilized 'natural resources' because these animals are every bit as capable of
having deep, meaningful connections with people. *Cow Hug Therapy* clearly demonstrates their advanced emotional and intellectual intelligence, as well as their resilience. I was most moved by Ellie's personal stories that involved people experiencing
or overcoming severe hardship forming bonds with animals that also had abusive
pasts. This read is perfect for anyone who appreciates being reminded of what's really
important in life. At the very least, it clearly demonstrates why all our domesticated
animals deserve to live humane lives."

— **Evan Antin**, DVM

"Many years ago, when my daughter was about three years old, we went to the Gentle
Barn for the first time. We had heard so many wonderful things about this sanctuary,
but I don't think any of us knew what we would experience. A peacock hanging with
pigs and llamas and sheep — I was blown away! But the thing that has stuck with me,
and why we go back so much, is cow hugging. At first, I was trepidatious because
they were so large and powerful...yet they're gentle. Ellie said, 'Lay your heart on
them,' and I felt a sense of calm I had never felt in my life. I've had a lot of traumas,

but at that moment, my heartbeat matched their rhythm, and I could breathe. The most amazing moment, however, was watching my tiny daughter who has a lot of energy and ADHD. She lay upon one of the cows and closed her eyes, and she was at peace. So for the past ten years, we have gone to the Gentle Barn whenever possible, especially when feeling lost, scared, or sad, and we know that these moments heal our hearts. Ellie and Jay and all the volunteers at the Gentle Barn have dedicated their lives not only to loving and caring for these incredible animals, but to caring for us as well. Dare I say they're angels? I was recently diagnosed with MS, and we made a trip there, and I actually left walking better. Thank you, cows. This book shows not only the power of Cow Hug Therapy with these wonderful creatures, but also their beautiful, individual personalities, which are evident when you meet them. I hope this book shows you how much of a blessing cows — and all creatures — are to our planet."

— **Christina Applegate**

"I love animals, and, like Ellie Laks, I want to see a world where animals can live their own lives, free from human harm. Ellie's book gives us the reasons why this is necessary and possible. In the stories of her rescued animals, it is clear that they have personalities, intelligence, and the capacity for profound emotions. The remarkable animals in her book teach us how to be better and happier humans. *Cow Hug Therapy* helps us all fall more deeply in love with animals, life, and ourselves. It's a must-read for anyone who loves animals like I do, or for anyone walking their own path of self-discovery. I have been to the Gentle Barn many times and leave feeling more uplifted every time. This book is like a private tour of the Gentle Barn and a love story about these animals, all of whom are majestic, wise healers."

— **Moby**

"Nonhuman animals need all the help they can get in an increasingly human-dominated world. The animals at the Gentle Barn are most fortunate to have Ellie Laks and her dedicated and tireless coworkers take care of them and give them a voice and much better lives than they previously had. Cows are highly emotional and sentient beings who deserve to be treated with dignity, compassion, and respect. *Cow Hug Therapy* clearly shows that when we care for other animals and honor who they are and what they need, we also profit, a win-win for all. This is a wonderful book and I hope it enjoys a global audience because its main messages and life lessons also apply to countless other animals who are used and abused in the name of humans."

— **Marc Bekoff**, PhD, University of Colorado, author of
Dogs Demystified and *The Emotional Lives of Animals*

Cow Hug Therapy

Cow Hug Therapy

How the Animals at the Gentle Barn Taught Me about Life, Death, and Everything in Between

Ellie Laks

Illustrations by Val Smith

New World Library
Novato, California

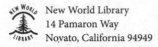

New World Library
14 Pamaron Way
Novato, California 94949

Cover photos copyright © the Gentle Barn

Text design by Tona Pearce Myers

Library of Congress Cataloging-in-Publication Data

Names: Laks, Ellie, author.
Title: Cow hug therapy : how the animals at the Gentle Barn taught me about life, death, and everything in between / Ellie Laks.
Description: Novato, California : New World Library, [2024] | Summary: "The inspirational story of the rescued animals of the Gentle Barn Foundation and how they became a therapeutic salve for countless guests from all over the world. The author brings their personalities to life and finds uplifting lessons in their individual stories"-- Provided by publisher.
Identifiers: LCCN 2024002619 (print) | LCCN 2024002620 (ebook) | ISBN 9781608688685 (paperback) | ISBN 9781608688692 (epub)
Subjects: LCSH: Animals--Therapeutic use--California. | Human-animal relation-ships--California. | Animal shelters--California. | Animal rescue--California. | Gentle Barn (Organization : Santa Clarita, Calif.) | Laks, Ellie.
Classification: LCC RM931.A65 L35 2024 (print) | LCC RM931.A65 (ebook) | DDC 615.8/5158--dc23/eng/20240311
LC record available at https://lccn.loc.gov/2024002619
LC ebook record available at https://lccn.loc.gov/2024002620

First printing, May 2024
ISBN 978-1-60868-868-5
Ebook ISBN 978-1-60868-869-2
Printed in Canada on 100% postconsumer-waste recycled paper

New World Library is proud to be a Gold Certified Environmentally Responsible Publisher. Publisher certification awarded by Green Press Initiative.

10 9 8 7 6 5 4 3 2 1

CONTENTS

INTRODUCTION

The fate of animals is of greater importance to me
than the fear of appearing ridiculous;
it is indissolubly connected with the fate of men.

— EMILE ZOLA

A s a child, I felt most comfortable around animals and out
in nature. I averted my eyes around other people, my
head hung low. I had no concept of who I was, or any sense of
self-esteem. I wasn't comfortable in my body, and my mind was
constantly filled with thoughts and fears that I couldn't control.
My emotions were mutable, depending on what was going on
around me. If I sensed people were pleased, then I was happy. If
there was discord with anyone else, I would feel upset and sad.
Even as a young adult, I did not know how to maintain my own
center and could only marvel at those who could.

I was born an animal lover and animal communicator.
From my earliest memory, I knew my connection with animals
was the pulse that circulated a life force inside me. Animals
called to me from the woods and lakes near my childhood
home. As a toddler, I would wander barefoot out of my house
to sit under a tree, where wild bunnies would hop up and sniff
at my open hands. One day when I was six, I was playing with
dolls in my room when I sensed the distressed call of a bird.

1

Though I couldn't hear it, I somehow knew where it was and ran down to the lake, where I found a baby bird who had fallen from a very tall tree. I could not find her nest, so I carried her home, created bedding in a nest shaped from grasses and mud, and fed her until the day she became strong enough to fly away.

I saw animals as my greatest teachers, healers, witnesses, and friends, while the people around me seemed to think of animals as things to eat, wear, and throw away when they didn't want them anymore. They couldn't see animals in the way that I did, and this perplexed me and made me heavyhearted.

My commitment at a very young age to always love and protect animals and my ability to understand them seemed to make other people uncomfortable. When I refused to dissect a frog at school or cried at Western movies when the horse got injured, they'd tell me that I was "acting crazy" or "being ridiculous." People would try to shape me into an image of their own making, and this only made me feel more different. I was lonely around other people and spent hours with my dog, my parakeet, and the woodland animals around my home. At age seven, I began to dream of a future where I lived on a big property, full of animals, and could show the world how beautiful they are.

When I finally founded the Gentle Barn in 1999, I wanted to help as many animals and people as possible. I knew that to reach that goal, I would have to get out of my own way by healing my low self-esteem issues and being my true self. The healthier I could become, the more animals I could save, people I could help, and Gentle Barn locations I could open. This is still a work in progress.

I have sought out many qualified therapists and healers over the years, but it has been my rescued animals that have taught me the most about myself and about life. They have no certificates, diplomas, or graduate degrees. They've never studied how to help people heal. They don't keep records or files. And yet they know what is needed. Animals have the wisdom of the Universe, pure instincts not harnessed by society's ideas of who and what is acceptable. They have loved me, raised me, and healed me. They have listened as I cried, accepted me as I was, and mirrored back to me that I am lovable. I always knew that I would spend my whole life saving animals, but I did not know that in return, they would save my life in such a profound way.

After twenty-three years at the Gentle Barn, I have witnessed and experienced things that most people have never had the chance to see. I have observed the instincts, intuition, and rituals of animals as they live through each of life's major themes — birth, love, finding purpose, healing, and death — and I want to share these gifts with you.

This isn't a scientific book, quoting studies to prove that cows have intelligence and feel emotions. After spending over two decades with them, every day, I absolutely know they do! To me, the idea that animals are less than or different than we humans, as fellow living beings, is offensive. Each one of the thousands of animals we have rescued and rehabilitated through the Gentle Barn has taught me, in their own way, that we are all the same in our hearts, no matter what we look like on the outside. We each feel happy and sad at times and feel fear for the same reasons. We each experience love and a sense of belonging with our family and friends, and we all hope for a good life. I trust that you'll come to your own conclusions about the intelligence and affection of animals after reading about the experiences I'm honored to share with you in this book.

Every single animal has so much to offer and teach us! Horses teach us strength and leadership, and smaller animals help us practice empathy. While I deeply love all of our animals, this book will focus mostly on cows.

Cows offer us something unique and special. They are huge animals, so we cannot really *make* them do anything, yet they are gentle, kind, and nurturing when they include us in their family. When they feel safe, they offer themselves up to love and heal us. The cows we have rescued and have had the privilege of knowing at the Gentle Barn have taught me my most valuable lessons about life, death, and everything in between.

Cows are everything that people should be and, I hope, will be one day, when we fully awaken to love. Cows live together in a matriarchal family, led by the oldest and wisest female. She helps raise the babies, disciplines the teenagers, grooms each member of her family every morning, and stays by their side as they leave their bodies behind. Cows are vegan and harm no other living being. Even their teeth and feet are designed to be gentle on the earth, leaving the pastures and fields the way they found them. Cows meditate every single day, connecting to themselves and to each other. They face their troubles head-on and problem solve their way around them. While some of our other animal species might initially reject newcomers out of fear and can even react in a violent way, cows are 100 percent inclusive, accepting anyone into their herd. Devotion to family and community is their most valued ethic. And while they are affectionate with each other, they practice self-care every day, with an instinctual sense of well-being.

Our economic and agricultural systems have labeled cows in ways that make it easier to define their economic worth to people. A *heifer* is a young female who has not yet been bred.

Her young age is of value, yet her worth as a breeder has not yet been proven. A *bull* is an unneutered male who can be used for breeding. A *steer* is a neutered male who cannot be used for breeding and is valued only for his flesh.

I am not interested in definitions of any animal's economic value. My focus will always be on an upcoming world where we will no longer categorize and label species according to their monetary worth but rather treat them as cherished family members or neighbors with whom we share this planet. Each and every cow we have ever rescued was and is a treasured friend and partner, considered family. No matter what their gender is, I refer to them all as *cows*. Beyond that, I'll write about each cow using their given name.

My first book, *My Gentle Barn: Creating a Sanctuary Where Animals Heal and Children Learn to Hope,* offers deeper insight into my childhood, how animals saved me, and why I wanted to dedicate my life to saving them. The history of my early years of rescuing and saving animals and creating our successful social work programs, along with the story of how I met and fell in love with my husband Jay and how we joined forces to expand our mission, is also in my first book, which introduces worldwide readers to the Gentle Barn.

Cow Hug Therapy is about the lessons learned from animals, lessons that have shaped me and given me clarity on what matters most and the focus that propels me to offer their wisdom and hope to other people. I feel privileged to watch the way the Gentle Barn animals, especially the cows, bring healing to so many people. (Note: I have changed the names of certain people to protect their privacy.) I am encouraged by the great love and growing concern that people around the world feel for the animals with whom we share this planet. Animals, especially those we personally care for, bring us natural joy and friendship, and through their freely offered love, they heal the wounds we receive in our desperate human struggle to find our place and our purpose in this life. Even if you never have the opportunity to rest against the side of one of our Gentle Barn cows, the stories in this book will provide a simple guide for mental health, self-care, recovering from grief, and overall well-being.

CHAPTER ONE

KARMA

There is no such thing as death. Our loved ones step out
of their bodies, but they are always with us.

— KARMA

I am sitting cross-legged on the ground, as motionless as possible. All around me, in every direction, are huge animals. Each one outweighs me six or seven times over. One by one, the animals lower themselves to the ground. I can tell they are signaling each other, sharing instinctual messages of what to do. I can hear their deep, methodical breathing. I close my eyes, not out of fear, but to join them. I am meditating with my cows.

On this early summer morning, the cows and I are uniting to give our energy to a young woman — let's call her "Beth" — who is visiting the Gentle Barn for Cow Hug Therapy. Beth is leaning against our matriarch, Karma, the aged and wise leader of this family of cows. Beth is emotionally exhausted from a great loss in her life, and Karma's maternal energy encircles her heartbreak. Words are not needed. Karma has unconditional acceptance and restoration to offer. It is healing.

Karma voluntarily chose to do Cow Hug Therapy with hurting humans because she wanted to give back and pay it forward. The trauma and great losses she endured in her first years of life could have easily crushed her spirit. I changed her life for the better, and she forever changed mine, beginning with the day she arrived at the Gentle Barn in November of 2010.

In the world of rescue, basic needs always come first: clean water, fresh food, and warm shelter. It's true for people and it's true for animals. That fall, we were preparing for the new cows we were rescuing. Fresh hay was stocked in giant bins alongside a tank of clean, cool water, a bed of straw filled the cowshed, and there was plenty of outdoor space in the pasture, layered with soft sand.

A few days before, my husband Jay and I had decided to rescue four turkeys being raised to slaughter for Thanksgiving dinner. When Jay went to pick up the turkeys, he was stunned by the brutal conditions a herd of eight cows were living in on the same property. Everywhere Jay looked was trauma, neglect, borderline starvation, and impending death.

Once the turkeys were safe in our care, we couldn't shake the sorrow of knowing other animals were living in cruel conditions mere miles from our sanctuary. We called our local animal control office to describe conditions on the farm and ask them for help. Knowing that the help from animal control would come slowly, Jay hooked up a trailer to his truck the next day and went back to rescue the first two cows, who were barely surviving. When they arrived, I promised them, as I do at every animal's arrival to the Gentle Barn, that they would never be mistreated again. All their needs would be met, with respect and abundant love.

Any expectation of kindness from human beings had been destroyed, however, and at first our new arrivals were very wary of Jay and me. The malnourished black and white dairy cow took in her new situation and seemed to relax as she hungrily munched all the hay she wanted. Within a few hours her face looked much softer. I gave her the name Shanti, which means *peace*.

The second cow, a small auburn Hereford with a white and freckled face, huge dark eyes, long eyelashes, fuzzy teddy bear ears, and a puppy dog nose, reacted in a way we didn't expect. She anxiously paced the pen, tipping her head upward and calling with a mournful cry, hour after hour. No one could figure out what was wrong with her, including our veterinarian.

The next morning, at dawn, I went back to the pen because her haunting cries had echoed across the barnyard most of the night. Her agony was breaking my heart.

"What is it, my darling?" I spoke softly, leaning on the top rail of the gate. "What do you need? I'll help you."

It was then that I noticed the milk dripping from her udder. Cows produce milk only if they have given birth. The cause of her sorrow now seemed so obvious that I couldn't believe I hadn't figured it out before. I hurried back to the house.

"Jay, she is crying for a baby!"

Jay told me he hadn't seen any new calves in that deplorable situation, but he picked up the phone and called the property owner, who begrudgingly admitted that he had hidden the calf the day before. He explained that the baby had already been sold to someone for Christmas dinner. He was supposed to deliver the calf that day, except his truck had broken down.

Without hesitating, Jay hooked up the trailer to his truck and drove quickly back to the property. When he arrived, the property owner and a few other men were standing on a long, sloping driveway next to their truck, which couldn't be shifted into drive. The little calf was tied up in the back, trembling. The men were frustrated and not at all happy to see Jay again.

If, as the adage goes, "Necessity is the mother of invention," then the "Father of figuring it out" is Jay. He knew that if a truck is parked on an uphill slope without the parking brake engaged, its gears will seize up. He knew that's what had happened here, and he knew the other men did not.

"How about this?" Jay asked, casually befriending them. "I'll fix your truck right now, and you'll give me the calf." The property owners scoffed. Thinking they had tried everything to get the truck into gear already and not thinking Jay could help, they shook hands with Jay, agreeing to the exchange.

Jay then used his truck to tow theirs up the hill about three feet, which loosened the gearbox, making it possible to shift into drive. He had fixed it. The owner was not happy but honored the handshake, and the calf was ours.

After eighteen hours of pacing and crying for her missing calf, the beautiful red cow had finally sunk to the ground in defeat, her head drooped, her eyes closed. She wouldn't eat or drink water. When she heard Jay's truck pull onto the property, she instinctively got back on her feet and began calling out to her baby, sensing her calf was nearby.

The tiny cinnamon-colored calf was led off the trailer, weak and shaky, as if these were the final steps to his death. When he was brought out into the open, his mom extended her head between the fence rails, eager to be reunited with him. The little calf felt such relief at seeing his mother again that he passed out at her feet. She sniffed and licked him, making soft low moos and nudging him gently with her nose until he recovered and stood up. She licked him all over until he was soaking wet, and then, shaking with joy, he began to nurse. The mom let out a loud sigh of relief and never made another sound of distress again.

I watched the reunion of mother and child while holding my own baby daughter Cheyanne in my arms, and tears ran down my face. It is illegal for anyone to take my child away from me, yet this cow's baby was stripped away from her without a second thought. As happy as I was to reunite this pair, I knew this forced separation happens to millions of cows around the world, every single day.

I hugged Jay for having the determination to make this happen for our new cow, and I thanked her for being vocal and persistent about letting us know her baby had been taken from her. I decided to name her Karma, as she had shaped her own destiny and that of her son.

Over the following months, we scraped together the resources to rescue the other six cows from that awful place. They were extremely skittish and fearful and would run to the other side of the pasture if any humans approached them. Every day

I would sing to them or read out loud, until they eventually began to trust. Still, it took Karma months to fully believe that her calf, whom we named Mr. Rojas, would not be kidnapped again. We kept reassuring her that her baby was hers for the rest of her life and that we would always respect her. In time, as her son grew, she came to trust us. Karma gradually took her place as the matriarch of the family and led the way until all the others lowered their guards and began to live in trust that they would be safe in their new forever home.

Eventually this little group of cows created a comfortable routine. They woke up with the sunrise and ate breakfast side by side. Afterward, they stood in a circle and groomed each other with their tongues. Usually, Karma licked every cow in the herd until their coats glistened and rippled in a cowlick pattern. Then, they all lay down and closed their eyes. Their faces took on a dreamy, relaxed look as they rhythmically chewed their cuds for over an hour, female and male, young and old, in a group meditation.

Seven or eight months after we brought Karma home to the Gentle Barn, an animal care staff member came to me at the end of a long day, saying that Karma's udders were swollen. "Does she have an infection?" I asked.

"I think she is about to give birth," he answered.

"That can't be possible," I reasoned. "She had a tiny nursing calf when we brought her here. Surely, they would not have impregnated her that soon after giving birth?!"

Every night before I go to bed, I make one last round through the barnyard to make sure everyone is safe and happy for the night. I tuck the pigs into bed with blankets, count the chickens and turkeys to ensure they are all safely on their roosts, give Sun Chlorella Rejuv-A-Wafer treats to each sheep, goat, and llama, and bring bedtime cookies to the horses and cows. That night, Karma was standing at the fence as I approached, her eyes on me, which was unusual. I could tell that she wanted my attention.

"Karma, are you all right?"

As soon as I got closer to the fence, Karma turned around to show me a tiny hoof and part of a leg beginning its entrance into the world.

I ran back up to the house as fast as I could. Jay and our children, Jesse, Molli, and Cheyanne, were all sound asleep in their own rooms.

"Wake up," I called as I ran up the stairs and caught my breath. "We're having a baby!"

By the time I returned to the cow pasture with my sleepy family, Karma was in full labor. To our amazement, every single cow had formed a circle around her and stood silently by, watching her. We found our place in the circle and joined them as Karma labored, pushed, and delivered her baby.

When the baby arrived, he lay on the ground, vulnerable and wet. Karma cleaned him up from his nose to his tail and then let him dry off. We watched as the baby practiced rising to his feet, over and over, eventually toddling around Karma and figuring out how to nurse. The process took two hours, and none of us moved.

When the newborn had his fill of his mother's milk, he lay down to sleep off the exhausting process of birth as Karma stayed next to him. It was only then that the circle of cows took on a different form. Without confusion or conflict, they broke the circle and lined up in an orderly single file, the matriarchs and elders in front, and the young, more submissive cows in the back. The first cow in the line stepped up to sniff and greet the newborn calf and welcome him to the family. When she had finished, she stepped away and the second cow came forward. One by one, each member of our cow family greeted the new arrival with affection, inhaling his scent and giving him licks of welcome. After all the cows had taken their turn with the new baby, Jay, the kids, and I took our turn welcoming him and congratulating Karma.

As the lustrous moonlight spilled over us, we watched the baby sleep, smiling at how extraordinary life can be in its most surprising moments. It seemed only fitting that Karma's new son should be named Surprise.

Karma oversaw her family of cows while she nurtured and raised her two sons, never separating from them. By the time Surprise was a year old, he was much bigger than his mom and had to practically lie down and roll over to nurse. It was a spectacle! Our veterinarians at the time urged us to wean and separate Surprise from his mom. But I believed in Karma's wisdom. She knew what was right for her body and her baby, and I was not willing to tell her how to mother. Karma nursed Surprise until he was five years old, each time with a smile and look of bliss on her face. Perhaps she knew he was her very last baby and wanted to enjoy him for as long as she could.

A cow's natural life span is about ten to twenty years, often determined by their physical size. As with dogs, the larger cows are, the shorter their life span, while the smaller they are, the longer they will live. Karma was very small, but her sons were giants and towered over her. Eventually, she outlived both Surprise and Mr. Rojas.

By the time Surprise was eight years old, he could no longer stand or walk because of his size. Even though it was hard to say goodbye, we knew he had led a happy life. Born at the Gentle Barn, he had never known cruelty or hunger and was never treated like a product instead of a being. He left with as much support as he had received the day Karma gave birth to him, surrounded with love.

Mr. Rojas was in his ninth year when he signaled to us that he was miserable and ready to leave. Karma stayed by his side, calmly licking him. She watched as his breathing slowed and then stopped, her head bent low near to his, showing no fear.

In the weeks that followed, that same family of cows encircled Karma once again as she silently grieved her loss. They ate by her side, laid next to her to rest, and encircled her with their strength, nurturing, and healing. Eventually Karma moved forward, taking her sons' memory with her.

Karma continued to be a steady presence, a calm and strong leader who helped the other cows heal from past traumas as well as partnering with me to help humans heal. As she got older, we brought her down to the Gentle Barn's main property, to live in a much smaller and softer environment with a few of our other senior cows. They had all volunteered to interact with the public during our open barnyard Sundays. These were the cows who found purpose in giving healing love to our visitors.

One morning at the height of the Covid pandemic, a young woman arrived for Cow Hug Therapy. Our guest and Karma had a lot in common, so I knew it would be a healing match.

Beth and her partner had recently welcomed their first child, a perfect baby boy. Life was blissful, until one day she found her two-month-old baby lifeless in his bassinet. Devastated, she couldn't return to any semblance of her previous life, even after months of talk therapy and other healing techniques. Beth's mother became increasingly worried because her daughter appeared to be sliding into a dark isolation, unable to function. Her therapist recommended that she volunteer at the Gentle Barn, knowing that working with animals can be very healing to someone in an emotional crisis. After I heard her story, I assured Beth that I would be happy to have her volunteer, but first I wanted to invite her to come for a session of

Cow Hug Therapy as my guest. She agreed, telling me, "I have to dedicate myself to healing. I have to find a way to live again."

I introduced Beth to Karma. I demonstrated for the young woman how she could lean into Karma, feel her heartbeat, and sync with her slow, deep breathing. She didn't need to do anything except relax. I let her know that I would stay nearby in case she needed anything.

Sitting on the ground at Karma's shoulder, the grieving young mom leaned her back against Karma's side and closed her eyes. I watched as Karma encircled Beth with her body. To my amazement, every single cow, one by one, came over and joined Karma until Beth was in the center of their circle. The cows all closed their eyes and began to rhythmically chew their cuds. I too closed my eyes and joined their meditation, visualizing a restorative peace for the young mother. We all held that space for forty-five minutes; no one moved.

When Beth finally opened her eyes, she was astonished and then touched that the entire family of cows was participating in her healing. She looked around at all of us and smiled for the first time. She began telling stories about her baby and his brief time on earth as we all listened.

The next week, Beth's mother called to thank me. Her daughter seemed to have finally turned a corner from hopelessness to slowly crawling her way toward the future. When I next spoke to Beth about a year later, she was pregnant again with a baby girl and was devoting her time to helping other parents through the crisis of losing a child.

Karma taught me and many others that life, in its own brilliant way, gives us circumstances that may be out of our control, passages of time when we suffer and feel lost. Eventually, when we remember who we are and why we are here, we can use our experience to help others. This transformation is often the result of our hard work and perseverance in changing our trauma into a gift.

This is the circle of healing that happens every day at the Gentle Barn. Because of the difficulties of my own childhood, I founded the Gentle Barn to rescue animals from trauma. Once the animals recover and learn to trust, they pay it forward to people who are suffering the same stories of trauma, to help them recover and trust. They, in turn, have the chance to pay it forward to others who need a helping hand.

We all have a story, and throughout our lives we work to evolve, create, and offer up something of ourselves to the world. The sooner we heal ourselves, the sooner we can pay it forward and widen the ripple effect of kindness, opening people's hearts, connecting more deeply with each other, and creating a planet that is peaceful for humans and animals alike.

As the Covid pandemic grew from a brief quarantine of two weeks to a roller coaster of incalculable loss, depression, loneliness, and stress in its second year, I knew that the overall benefits of Cow Hug Therapy needed to be offered as a means of coping. We featured it on our website, and people signed up. They came to the Gentle Barn to be nurtured in the safest environment possible.

Word of mouth about the extraordinary calming effects of Cow Hug Therapy began to spread, and soon members of the press came calling, wanting to see for themselves. They were merely curious at first, thinking it would make a funny or quirky news story. Many of the journalists had never been up close to a cow before and arrived for their interviews with lighthearted humor and a play on words, like "In today's moos" and "Therapy like no udder." Yet they each left with a different perspective after becoming absorbed in the calming warmth of Cow Hug Therapy. Even the most skeptical left with an understanding of how being close to the large, warm, accepting presence of a cow could provide a stress-free, healing atmosphere to those who need unconditional acceptance to face whatever they are going through.

A few months before her tenth anniversary at the Gentle Barn, my wonderful Karma, almost twenty-seven years old and being treated for kidney failure, let me know she was ready to pass the title of matriarch to the next in line, a majestic black and white Holstein named Crystal. Every day, Karma and Crystal would go into the barn together by themselves and lie down, face to face, as Karma seemed to transfer her wisdom to Crystal.

On the day Karma passed away, I held her head in my lap, thanking her for the teacher, role model, and healing inspiration she had been. I could feel her joy as her spirit drifted upward, toward her future. I knew it was a goodbye only in the physical form, but as I walked slowly back up the hill to the house, I shed many tears at the thought of a future without Karma's hugs. By watching Karma lead, live, and parent her babies, I had grown into the mother, grandmother, wife, teacher, and leader I had wanted to be.

In her final years, Karma had helped me bring Cow Hug Therapy to hurting human beings and even into the national spotlight. As I moved her story and photo into the Memoriam page of the Gentle Barn website, I looked at her kind and wise face and thought, "What a life well lived!" A life that truly did create a new destiny for the Gentle Barn.

CHAPTER TWO

BUDDHA

We are not our circumstances, our bodies, or our pain.
We are much greater than that!

— BUDDHA

While Karma hosted Cow Hug Therapy beautifully for hurting individuals after the pandemic, she wasn't the one who invented it. Cow Hug Therapy was created almost two decades earlier by a miniature cow named Buddha.

Buddha was a fuzzy, red, eight-hundred-pound cow with a white face, teddy bear ears, and a pink nose. Before I rescued her, Buddha was part of a miniature cow breeding program. Because she could not get pregnant and earn her keep, she was being sent to slaughter. Thankfully I was able to bring her home to me instead. From the minute I met her, I knew she was no ordinary cow. Alert ears framed curly bangs on top of her head, and long, white ringlets coiled at the end of her tail. She looked at me with giant eyes, lashes fluttering like butterflies, and I felt she was gazing into my soul. Compared to many previous animals I had rescued who were terrified and untrusting, Buddha arrived in the quiet of our barnyard open, affectionate, at ease, and inviting from day one. I wondered what Buddha's reaction would be on her first open Sunday, when many guests came to meet our animals at the Gentle Barn.

I founded the Gentle Barn in 1999, after dreaming about it since childhood. Animals had always been the ones I cried to, the ones who listened. They were the ones who mirrored back to me that I was wanted and lovable when I didn't feel that way about myself. And it was animals who encouraged me to keep going when I didn't want to be here. From the time I was seven I would tell anyone who would listen that when I grew up, I would have a big place full of animals and show the world how beautiful they are.

I finally opened the first Gentle Barn in my half-acre back-yard after bringing home sick animals from an abusive petting zoo. Since then, we have opened locations in Nashville, Tennessee, and St. Louis, Missouri, as well. We rescue severely abused and neglected animals who have nowhere else to go and re-habilitate them using veterinary care, chiropractic treatments, acupuncture, deep tissue massage therapy, holding therapy, music therapy, animal communication, nutritional supple-ments, energy healing, and lots of love.

Once the animals are happy, healthy, and ready, we part-ner with them to heal people with similar stories of trauma, connecting people to the love and magic of animals. We are open to the public on Sundays so guests can hug cows, cuddle turkeys, cradle chickens in their arms, give pigs tummy rubs, pat goats, feed horses carrots, and so much more. During the week we host school field trips, private tours, and gentle birth-day parties and offer our animal-assisted therapy programs for people who come looking for hope.

We had about one hundred visitors on Buddha's first open Sunday. Buddha watched as the first wave of people entered the barnyard, but she didn't move away or resist the attention. Instead, she inserted herself into the middle of the crowd and lay down, inviting people to brush, hug, and cuddle with her. I couldn't believe it. Tears stung my eyes and my mouth opened in awe as I watched my new cow while toddlers wrapped their arms around her neck for a cuddle and adults rested their faces against her curly, red coat, smiling from ear to ear. I was ready to whisk her away into the privacy of our backyard if it seemed the crowds would upset her, but Buddha instinctively under-stood the mission of the Gentle Barn and wanted to help.

After dinner that evening, I put one-year-old Jesse to bed and headed out to do one more routine check on the barnyard before my own bedtime. Everyone there was tucked into their straw beds or roosting in the rafters, a soothing hum audible as the animals snored softly in unison. Only Buddha was awake, watching me from the barnyard corner as I checked on the other animals. She seemed to be beckoning me over. I was going to give her a quick pat on the head as I passed by, but something made me stop. She looked up at me as if she needed more. I kneeled, then sat on the ground and allowed Buddha to have my weight as I leaned gently on her. All day long I had been stoic, focused on my to-do list, but at that moment the extent of my exhaustion hit me, and I sank fully into her. Resting my face on her side, I closed my eyes and sighed out the stress of the day. Then something extraordinary happened that would change my life and my work: Buddha wrapped her neck around me and gave me a hug.

Turkeys and chickens had often settled into my arms as I held them, dogs usually followed me around, horses stood still when I groomed them, and sheep and goats would brush up against my legs for treats and pats. This was different. It was a cow, and she was hugging me. Buddha wasn't only taking my affection — she was caring for me in return! Her gesture moved me so deeply, I wept into her shoulder, completely forgetting that my husband was waiting for me. I forgot about everything: the day, my responsibilities, everything. My thoughts stopped swirling, and my mind completely relaxed. Buddha and I were silent together under the night sky, as if covered in a dome where only peace existed. All I was aware of was the calming thump of her heartbeat in my ear and the rise and fall of her breathing. I could not remember the last time I was unconditionally hugged like that, and it filled me up. I felt small and vulnerable, and completely safe.

Buddha's bedtime hugs became a ritual. Sometimes when she was lying down, I would sit next to her for a few moments to rest my cheek against her fuzzy coat, close my eyes, breathe in and out, and exhale the day away. Other times, I would cry on her shoulder and talk out loud about whatever was complicated or a struggle. I would tell her my hopes. In response, she would hug me like a loving mom, and I would melt into her side. Those hugs filled me with hope and strength, and I would go to bed ready to rest and wake up the next day to work even harder. I came to rely on Buddha's therapeutic hugs, and I started wondering if other people needed cow hugs too.

Buddha's healing was very different from regular therapy. In traditional therapy, we talk about what we have been through, dissecting our feelings in a cognitive, left-brained way. We work to understand various life experiences in order to accept and apply the lessons they offered and the strength they gave us. That is helpful. In contrast, Buddha's Cow Hug Therapy allowed me to free my mind of thoughts, to let it rest by just being present for a while. It allowed me to feel grounded and humble, opening my right brain to healing without words. It made me feel renewed. It transformed me like no other mode of therapy or healing I had tried in the past.

I knew traditional talk therapy was not for everyone. Some of us don't want to relive our trauma, don't want to drag the past into the present. Some are too angry or shut down to talk about our experiences and feelings. Some find talk therapy helpful but are looking for something more. I was certain that Buddha's hugs could help others as much as they were helping me.

I contacted agencies that helped teenagers at risk, young adults on probation, teens and adults recovering from substance abuse, men and women experiencing homelessness, families at domestic violence shelters, service members at veterans' centers, and young children with special needs, and invited them to bring their clients to visit the animals. And they did. The number of groups coming to visit the Gentle Barn was growing by the minute, as was the number of visitors on open

Sundays. We now only had one rule at the Gentle Barn: everyone who visited had to get a hug from Buddha.

Before brushing the horses, holding the chickens, playing with the goats and sheep, and giving the pigs tummy rubs, every single visitor was brought to Buddha and shown how to rest their face on her, close their eyes, match the rise and fall of her breathing to theirs, and slow down their heartbeat to be in sync with hers. Time and time again, I watched as the experience transformed them. When people embraced and were embraced by Buddha, they were changed. I could see it in their faces. This was especially true for the teenagers and young adults going through hard times. They typically seemed defensive, cold, tough, and hardened at first, and they didn't want to hug Buddha. They didn't want to get their T-shirts or shoes dirty. They didn't want to be vulnerable or seem weak in front of their peers. But I just kept modeling it, kept talking about Buddha and her personality. Buddha and I were patient and persistent, and eventually even the most stubborn guest ended up getting a hug.

The minute they put their faces on Buddha's shoulders, I could see struggle melt into vulnerability, sweetness, and openness. They transformed into little kids right in front of me. It was like watching a miracle every time. After a Buddha hug, the rest of their visit was remarkable. The young men and women would suddenly look at me, ask questions, and become willing to get dirty, lie down on the ground with a pig, or hold a chicken in their arms. It opened them up like nothing else I've ever seen.

Buddha was transforming lives. She was opening people to who they truly were. She was teaching me how to do this work at the Gentle Barn, how to utilize interaction with animals to really benefit people long-term. Over the course of thirteen and a half years, Buddha and I hosted every Sunday and weekday group together. She gave out three hundred thousand hugs in her lifetime. Many visitors adopted a vegan diet after meeting Buddha. Mostly, though, she helped people find themselves, and few walked away without shedding tears of relief.

While Buddha was helping me host groups at the Gentle Barn, she also taught me to meditate. I wanted to commit myself more to my own mental health and thought meditation could be a good addition to my daily routine. I had been trying to meditate on my own, but my early attempts were excruciating. I struggled to sit still, clear my head, and stop the monkey chatter. I'd sit with my eyes closed, the whole time thinking, "Is it over yet? Is my alarm going to sound? I can't sit here anymore." It was really painful, but I persevered.

One night after making my barnyard rounds, I leaned in to hug Buddha, but this time, instead of embracing me, she shrugged me off and moved a few feet away. It was clear that she wasn't open for hugs. I still wanted to be in her company, so I sat where I was and closed my eyes. Without expecting to meditate, my mind emptied of its swirling thoughts and the brain waves slowed. I felt as peaceful as if I were hugging Buddha. She stayed nearby, completely still with her eyes closed, for about ten minutes. Afterward I felt refreshed, clear, and energized. From that evening on, Buddha beckoned me to sit next to her to meditate with her. I was able to clear my head, focus on my breath, hold still, and receive great ideas about the direction of the Gentle Barn. We meditated together for about ten to thirty minutes a day, depending on how much time I had. Though I didn't realize it at the time, Buddha was preparing me for a much bigger life lesson, one necessary to my continued mission at the Gentle Barn.

One day we received a call at the Gentle Barn office from a woman in Chicago who said she was an animal communicator and had been guided to move to California to work with me. I didn't formally believe in animal communication, though I, myself, had heard the voices of animals since early childhood. I asked my office assistant to please tell her, "No, thank you." Over the next several weeks the woman persistently called the office every single day, asking to meet with me.

The Gentle Barn had grown quite popular by then, and we had thousands of guests coming from all over the world. Had I attracted a stalker? I clearly had a decision to make. Should I get a restraining order, or should I invite her out to the Gentle Barn? Wanting to always act with love, I decided to meet with her.

I first met Amanda with apprehension, wanting to quickly discern whether she was a fake. What I experienced was the opposite: Amanda had gentle eyes and an enchanting smile, and I felt myself opening up to her sweet nature. By the time our meeting was over, it felt like we were old friends, and we agreed to start working together.

Over the next three years, Amanda helped me connect to that intuitive part of myself that I had known as a child, was teased for as a teenager, and didn't want to admit having as an adult. That gift had set me apart from other people, making me feel lonely, weird, and crazy, but Amanda helped me connect back to who I really was, made me feel proud of my gifts instead of ashamed and embarrassed, and helped me connect more deeply with the animals I was rescuing. Buddha and Amanda were both showing me that it was time to start embracing the real me.

It was right around the Gentle Barn's fourteenth anniversary that Buddha started having trouble. The tendons in her legs were shrinking, which left her legs unnaturally bent and made mobility difficult for her. She moved slowly and deliberately and spent more time lying down. I felt a desperate need to comfort her and brought in massage therapists, acupuncture professionals, and chiropractors to do treatments and hopefully ease any pain. Buddha allowed every treatment.

Through Amanda I was able to ask Buddha how she was feeling. Was she in pain? How else could I help her? Buddha would answer every question the same way, no matter how often I asked. "I'm not my body. The way you see me is not who I am. I can transcend pain. I can transcend my physical body. Please stop projecting suffering onto me. I'll let you know what I need when I need it, but please stop looking at me with all that concern on your face."

She repeated herself until I fully grasped the concept. Buddha was teaching me that our souls, our spirits, the essence of who we are, is much greater than the sum of our parts.

Yes, we have bodies, and yes, our bodies can have aches and pains, and yes, we all age. But our physicality is not who we are. Buddha was showing me that she didn't have to be defined by her physical circumstances. We are all far greater, brighter, and stronger than our physical form.

I wanted Buddha to remain in my day-to-day life as long as possible, so her attempts to enlighten me didn't change my actions. I continued to support her and provide her with every physical treatment I could find. At one point, Buddha made it clear to me that I was doing this for my own benefit, to make *myself* feel better. She did not define herself as one who was suffering and in need of care. I was the one who was suffering at the thought of losing her.

I know now that she was right. Giving her treatments did make me feel better and less hopeless. At least I was doing something. I just couldn't imagine the Gentle Barn without Buddha as my teacher and friend.

About a year later, I was in a board meeting with Jay and other board members, about thirty minutes from home. I had seen Buddha eat breakfast that morning and had animal care-takers holding the fort while I was gone. She'd seemed fine to me, and I had left for the meeting without worries. Focused on the discussion at hand, I was not thinking about Buddha at all when, all of a sudden, I heard her voice in my head saying, "It's time, you need to come home." My face went pale, and my eyes filled with tears. It must have looked like I'd seen a ghost because people in the meeting asked, "Ellie, what's the matter?" But I could not answer, I could not say a word. I excused my-self and walked out to the hallway, closed my eyes, and tried to connect with Buddha.

I heard her say, "You need to come home. It's time for me to transition."

I ran to my car and within moments was on the freeway, racing home, my hands trembling, hyperventilating as I drove. I had dreaded this day, knowing I would never be ready to live my life without Buddha, the rock of my life.

I began to doubt what I had heard. Maybe it was only my imagination, and Buddha was fine. I called Amanda and asked her to check in with Buddha, telling her nothing else. I told her I would stay on the line.

A few minutes later, Amanda was saying, "Ellie, I have some really bad news."

"What is it?" I asked, holding back sobs.

"Buddha's ready to transition."

I don't remember how I made it the rest of the way home, feeling it couldn't be true, but knowing it was.

I arrived at the Gentle Barn and walked quickly to the cow barn. Buddha looked up at me from where she lay in the barn, with that bright face she'd greeted me with a thousand times before, and said, "It's time."

Everything in me, every single, solitary cell in my body wanted to say, "No. No. Get up! Stand up. I need you! I need more time with you. You can't leave me."

Buddha gazed at me with steady, calm eyes until I could see that it would only disrespect her to not listen to her decision to leave her body. As I waited for the vet to arrive, I sat with Buddha and meditated with her one last time. She reminded me that a transition is not an ending, that our connection could never die; it would continue on in a different form, so I didn't need to feel afraid. She promised to never leave me. She said that she would always love me.

I stared into her face, trying to commit every curve, detail, and nuance to memory. I put my face into her fur and took in a long breath, locking into my senses her talcum powder scent. I took in the long, blond ringlets of her tail, the round curve of her hips, those fuzzy red ears that always made her look like a mythical creature. I rested my hands on the smooth, gray hooves that had held her up for so long but failed her today.

The vet arrived, and Jay ushered her into the barn, helped her set up the sedative shots, and stood by as they were administered. I couldn't look. I stared into Buddha's eyes as she rested her silky chin in my hands. Choking back sobs, I thanked her for being my greatest teacher, my partner, my friend, and for making the biggest difference in my life. I held her face, speaking of my love for her until she left her body.

When it was over, I thanked the vet. She gave Jay and me sympathetic hugs and left. Once her car pulled away, all the energy left my muscles; it was as if gravity pulled me to the ground under the weight of unbearable grief. I collapsed next to Buddha's lifeless body. I could hear screaming and crying and thought, "Who the hell is making such an awful noise?" Then I realized the mournful wails were coming from me. It was the terrible sound of horrific sorrow. Jay knelt next to me, not knowing what to do. I felt embarrassed and did not want my staff to hear me, but I couldn't stop. It was beyond my control.

I don't know how much time passed before Jay got me up off the ground and back home. My hair was covered in wood shavings, my eyes were swollen and puffy, and long tear marks ran down my dusty face. Once in our bedroom, I sank to the floor in a fetal position. I could not stop wailing. For the next two weeks I barely ate and slept fitfully off and on. The pain was so huge that I felt like I was going to die.

Jay finally called Amanda, as he no longer knew how to help me. Amanda came over and held me. She didn't try to stop me from crying, or to control my thoughts, or fix the way I was grieving. She simply sat next to me, mostly silent, and held space for me. She allowed me to go through my process and have my grief, and she stayed there as my witness. I'll forever be indebted to Amanda for her kindness and support that day.

A few weeks later, I was still inconsolable. Amanda asked, "Would you like me to speak to Buddha for you?" The minute I heard her say Buddha's name I felt the pain, like a slap in the face. I took a deep breath and answered with a silent nod. I didn't have the confidence to hear Buddha on my own. Besides, I think the pain would have drowned out her voice. But I so wanted to hear her. Amanda became the translator, from Buddha to me.

The first thing Buddha communicated through Amanda to me was, "Knock it off." She told me, "I see you crying. I've seen you lying on the floor. I see that you feel broken. But I'm still here with you. I didn't go anywhere. I'm right here with you.

Our connection will never die. Our love will never die. My life force didn't die. There's no such thing as death. I only stepped out of my body. The faster you realize that, the faster you can move forward."

Despite Buddha's clear message to me, I still wasn't doing well. I couldn't work. I couldn't stop crying, and on many days, I couldn't get out of bed.

Ever since I was a child, I related deeply to Native American cultures. I had no experience in Native cultures, being raised Orthodox Jewish with Eastern European DNA. However, from the time I could walk, I behaved in ways I imagined were somehow Native American. I grew my dark hair long, insisted on being barefoot, and spent hours galloping back and forth in my yard as if I were on a horse. I took decorative gourds and squashes from the house, cut them open and removed the insides, dried them in the sun, and used them as my drinking and eating utensils. To this day, people ask me if I am Native American. I always respond that in my soul, I absolutely am. So, when a California sect of the Yamassee Muscogee tribe offered to adopt us as part of their family, it was with a lot of enthusiasm that we said, "Yes, please!"

After I had suffered about a month of relentless grief, Jay asked some members of the tribe if they could somehow help me find a way out of my pain. The next day all the grandmothers of the tribe, about fifteen women, came to see me. They walked me up the back hill of our land in Santa Clarita, which I have always felt is sacred. There Jay had built a beautiful ceremonial firepit, already glowing red and orange. The women had me stand next to the fire and then formed a circle around me. They started singing traditional songs, and although I had never heard these songs before, they were familiar to me, as if I knew them from lifetimes past. When they finished singing, the grandmothers stood in front of me, one by one, and put sweet grapes and berries into my mouth. With the smoke from hand-held burning sage bundles, some of them brushed my hair and others did a full sweep of my body. They each took turns hugging me. No words, no discussion, no thoughts required. I felt like a child again, being cared for and nurtured, loved unconditionally. The ceremony took about an hour, by which time the fire had gone out, leaving wisps of smoke that curled, danced, and wound their way into the air. The matriarch grandmother took the extinguished coals from the fire and put them into a beautiful pouch, which she then strung around my neck. I was to wear this every day to connect me back to Buddha, to the circle of grandmothers and their unconditional love, and to the salve that they put on my heart that day.

Indigenous peoples have always healed grief communally, coming together in ceremony and song. It's a part of their cultures that they pass on from generation to generation. Western cultures have tragically lost those traditions. In US culture, for example, we are expected to return to work after a loss, especially if it is the loss of an animal. It is considered shameful to cry in public. In Western cultures we don't speak often of our feelings. We are expected to hold our emotions inside. Grief in our cultures is often taboo, lonely, and awkward. Many of us feel the need to hide our grief over losing an animal for fear of being teased or mocked about the length and depth of our sorrow. Or we may find that people are impatient if we still grieve after a day or two.

Grief can be so isolating. That's why it's important to create friendships and connections with those who will take our pain seriously, treat it as precious, and support us. Whether or not there are people around who support us, we can hold sacred space for ourselves to grieve. We can take the time to reflect and mourn, respecting the pain we feel. We can feed ourselves nourishing food, take bubble baths, walk in nature, and get lots of rest. We don't have to run from our grief. We can take our time and recover slowly.

Today I am a professional animal communicator. From my earliest memories, I have always heard the whispers of animals needing help or speaking to me about what they wanted. I have always been able to communicate with the rescued animals at the Gentle Barn and learn what they have gone through and what they need. Now I speak to animals on behalf of clients around the world so they can bond more deeply with their animals as well.

Engaging with animals who have transitioned is what I enjoy the most. I try to hold a sacred space for my clients, knowing that in their grief and agony, they may not have many places to turn. Their children might not understand the depths of their grief. Their partners might just want them to get over it already. They may not have friends they can turn to for the length and depth of their despair. I connect them back to their animal so that they know he or she never left them. I feel honored to relay messages and memories from the animal to my clients, to help them heal the way Amanda and the grandmothers did for me.

Buddha taught me that once our loved ones transition, the connection isn't over; it is only a different experience, with a different form. Instead of opening our eyes to see, smell, touch, and hold our loved ones, we can close our eyes and feel them with us.

Once I mourned the loss of our physical relationship and Amanda had reconnected me to Buddha, I learned to trust that Buddha was still with me. I was able to continue our meditations and connect with her every morning. I now understood the reason she kept me at arm's length toward the end of her life and taught me meditation. I now had a way to continue our communication and togetherness after she had transitioned. Time and time again, she offers the most profound, incredible, life-altering advice — better than any therapist, better than any business advisor. Anytime I have a challenge, she always answers. All I have to do is close my eyes, think of her, pose a question, and the answer comes. Buddha continues to this day to be my closest mentor, advisor, best friend, and teacher.

CHAPTER THREE

DUDLEY

We are all here for a greater purpose.
We must not be limited by what others think of us,
but rather must define ourselves
and show the world who we are.

— DUDLEY

There was a woman seated at the end of our bed. I didn't know how she got into our bedroom in the middle of the night, but I was very aware of her presence.

"Don't worry," she said in a loud, clear voice. "In exactly six months you will open your next Gentle Barn, and you will have the best two years of your life."

I rubbed my eyes, quickly sitting up in bed to try to understand who she was and what was happening. I couldn't believe that her voice didn't wake up Jay, who continued to snore melodically on his side of the bed. Even our small dogs, Bingo and Little One, were still asleep beside me. By the time my eyes were open enough to take in the entire room, no one was there.

I dismissed it all as a very realistic and vivid dream, but I was so intrigued by the clarity of the woman's message that I got up and wrote down her words in my journal, along with the date, December 15, 2014. Then I fell back asleep, and by the next day I'd forgotten all about it.

Up until this point, the Gentle Barn California had been rapidly growing in popularity, with thousands of social media followers added each month. Clients from community service agencies and rehab facilities would visit the location two to four times per week to interact with the animals. In my daily meditations with Buddha, I'd begun to get direct inspiration to open another Gentle Barn. I could feel an urgency behind it: the environment, the animals, and even humanity were running out of time to course-correct.

Jay and I looked into opportunities to open in other

states. A lovely couple in Hawaii wanted to partner with us, but when we found out that they only rented the land they were using for a sanctuary, we had to walk away — purchasing land there was not in our budget. We looked into opening in South Carolina, but the community we were working with had a population of only a few hundred people and it was too far off the grid to be effective and attract visitors. In addition, our board members were advising us that, financially, it wasn't the right time to create a second location. There were roadblocks at every turn, but I continued to receive the inspiration to find a second location. I had all the motivation needed, but no idea how to make it happen. Then the woman appeared in my bedroom.

The next month, in January, in anticipation of my upcoming birthday, I told Jay that I didn't want a party, gifts, or even a card. I wanted only one thing: to rescue a cow. Jay, who by this time was used to me saying things like this, nodded his OK. We thought we would find a cow that needed help somewhere in Los Angeles. A few days later we got a call from someone in Tennessee saying they knew of a cow who had lost a foot and was hobbling around on three legs. She said that the cow was in terrible pain and the people he was living with were going to send him to slaughter. She had made over two hundred phone calls all over the country trying to find someone to help this cow, and nobody could take him in. She said, "I know that you're really far away, and you probably can't do anything to help, but can you at least give me some advice?"

Remembering my birthday wish, Jay decided to see if it would be possible to help this poor injured cow even from two thousand miles away. Without me knowing, Jay researched bovine surgeons in the Tennessee area and found a leading one at the University of Tennessee Knoxville, about three hours from the ranch where the cow was living. Then he found a few companies that made prosthetics for animals.

A few days later Jay came to me and said, "Happy birthday! Surprise, we're going to Tennessee to rescue a cow!"

We flew into a snow-covered Nashville airport. We had left weather in the high 70s in Southern California, and the frigid air in Tennessee stung my throat and my breath came out in white puffs. As we walked to the rental car, I rubbed my gloved hands together for warmth and zipped my jacket up around my neck. Soon we were driving through flurry conditions on slippery roads until we reached the ranch.

The rancher met us in the drive as soon as we got out of the car. I thought I would have a difficult time relating to this man, who earned his living by exploiting animals to be sold as food. I was tempted to judge him, but when he warmly shook our hands, my predisposition fell away. I found myself drawn to his kind face, bright blue eyes, and inviting smile. After initial greetings and pleasantries, we went to the pasture behind his house to meet our new cow. Rounding the corner and seeing him for the very first time made me catch my breath and stopped me in my tracks. He looked identical to Buddha.

He was a small cow with fuzzy red fur, a wide white face, long white eyelashes, beautiful auburn teddy bear ears, and the cutest, softest pink puppy dog nose. I could see that he was in pain as he slowly hobbled toward us, trying to keep his weak, footless back leg from smashing into the frozen ground. The rancher explained that this cow, when younger, had baling wire accidentally wrapped around his leg. It had gone unnoticed in the large herd of cows, and eventually the lack of circulation caused his hoof and foot to break off completely. When it was time to sell the herd, the rancher didn't include this cow, who was disabled and in pain, but now he knew he couldn't keep him.

I approached this sweet-faced cow slowly, placing fresh grain on the ground before me. With an unsteady gait, he moved toward me, holding my gaze. When I looked into his eyes, I got chills all over and felt it was Buddha's eyes I was looking into. I dismissed that thought quickly — I wasn't sure I even believed in reincarnation in those days, and we had much more pressing things to focus on. So I set my heart on helping my new cow heal: we got him loaded on the trailer and to the hospital, over a hundred miles away.

We wanted him to have a name, right away, for his stay at the hospital. I knew his name should be warm, friendly, lighthearted, and approachable. He seemed to react well to "Dudley," and Jay and I loved it too.

Dudley spent the next five months at the University of Tennessee Knoxville Large Animal Hospital. He needed an amputation and several other surgeries to get his leg prepared for a prosthetic. He had underwater treadmill therapy to help him build back muscle strength; being held afloat by the water helped him exercise his legs without pain. He had acupuncture to increase circulation and decrease inflammation. He had chiropractic treatments to realign his spine. We gave him grain and Sun Chlorella to boost his immune system. We spent countless hours in the hospital reading and singing to Dudley, meditating with him, and bringing him treats. We soon discovered that his favorite was fresh peaches.

Finally, the day came when Ronnie from VIP Orthotics and Prosthetics delivered Dudley's new foot. Ronnie was smart, kind, and so knowledgeable, and Jay and I fell in love with him right away, and so did Dudley. An amputee himself, Ronnie had an inside angle on what the animals he treated were going through and feeling.

The prosthetic was a giant orange boot that opened like a clamshell. The back half went on first, with Dudley's residual limb fitting down into it. Then the other half fit in front. Once the front and back halves were in place, the prosthetic was held together by three wide black straps.

Ronnie showed us how to get Dudley acclimated to the prosthetic by putting it on for two hours, then taking it off for two hours. After a week, we increased to putting it on for three hours, and then having it off for one hour. By the third week, Dudley wore the prosthetic for four hours, and off for one hour, until he was able to wear it all day long and take it off only at night. We had to check his residual limb for sores, red spots, and blisters each time we took the prosthetic off. And we lathered his limb with Puremedy Healing Salve at night to keep his skin as healthy as it could be.

From the time Dudley was brought into the hospital to the day he was discharged five months later, we recorded and posted his experiences over live feeds on social media and YouTube. More and more viewers tuned in each day to watch his progress, and Dudley soon became world famous.

The world watched while Dudley was admitted into the hospital. They waited with me and Jay each time he was in surgery. They laughed with us when Dudley splashed water on his doctors from his underwater treadmill. They saw him receive treatments, try on his prosthetic for the first time, and nibble on bananas, oranges, and cookies. Millions of people were watching Dudley and rooting for him.

A member of the hospital staff kept a bag of peppermints in her desk. On her breaks she would visit Dudley and feed him peppermints. When Dudley's fans saw that on a live feed, they sent peppermints by the hundreds for Dudley. When the live feed showed Dudley shake his head in happy anticipation of a snack of fresh peaches, soon his new family of fans sent boxes of fresh peaches to the hospital. The growing number of viewers, willing to support our efforts, made me trust that we would be able to get a property and open a Gentle Barn in Tennessee, a place where Dudley could live close to his doctors. Jay and I proposed this idea to our board, and they agreed.

Without knowing Tennessee very well, we decided to rent a property, to give us time to find the right place. The only criteria: it had to be near the hospital. In a few weeks we found a twelve-acre property with a big barn and fenced pastures. It even came with a house across the street where we could stay when we visited and where our staff could live to keep an eye on things. It took us a few days to fit Dudley's stall, complete with a head gate to hold him still while we took his prosthetic on and off, but other than that, the property was turnkey.

Years prior we had rescued three horses from gross neglect in South Carolina, named Worthy, Indie, and Chris. Worthy was born with a deformed leg and needed major surgery in Kentucky. Once her operation and recovery were complete, we had boarded them all in Kentucky, where they were happy and could graze on endless green pastures. After finding the land to rent, we brought our horses home to Tennessee, where they settled in even before we picked up Dudley, the very next day.

I will never forget how Dudley stepped off the trailer, took in the wide span of open pastureland edged in wildflowers, sniffed at the ground, and then lifted his head up into the sun. In a flash, he realized his new mobility gave him freedom to move with joy for the very first time. He began jumping into the air, running straight, and then pivoting to go in a circle, around and around. The three horses came over to greet their new barn-mate and joined him in his joy, running around and around in the pasture until they were all worn out. Jay hugged me and we stood, watching the victory celebration and smiling until our faces ached. It was a great day!

We hired staff and brought in volunteers to keep Dudley and the horses comfortable and added other animals in need of rescue to our second location: three turkeys, two pigs, and some adorable chickens. These were even joined by a goat and a beagle who lived next door and belonged to the landlord. When they realized how much food, warmth, and attention they could get at the Gentle Barn, they moved right in.

Our opening day for the Gentle Barn in Tennessee was June 15, 2015, exactly six months after the dreamlike woman sat on the end of my bed and told me that my second Gentle Barn would be a reality in six months.

The media loved Dudley and was always hungry for stories about him. They came to witness his birthday party, complete with guests, gifts, and cake. They did a whole story about Dudley's love at first sight with Destiny. This small black cow had a bad shoulder injury, and we had saved her from impending slaughter. Though she was reluctant to let human hands touch her, Dudley taught her to trust people again and allow us to heal her. We even held a marriage ceremony for them. Dudley wore an orange bow tie, and Destiny was glammed up in a long white veil. Two hundred people gathered as they walked down the center aisle in the barn and I pronounced them safe, respected, loved, and together for the rest of their lives.

When the first group of amputees — women, men, and children — came to meet Dudley, the news programs wanted to be in on it too. Like Dudley, our guests had been through surgeries, rehabilitation, and the challenge of acclimating to prosthetics, and the cameras wanted to catch their reactions. Their faces lit up, their defenses lowered, and they could not help but be inspired by how joyous Dudley was, considering all that he had suffered. They wanted to know all about him, and I answered all their questions: How did Dudley protect his residual limb at night? What did he use for sores? Did he sweat under the prosthetic when it was hot out? As they listened to the answers, many nodded their heads in response, identifying with Dudley on common ground.

Word rapidly spread about Dudley, and the requests to meet him grew in number every week. Children in wheelchairs, kids born with differently formed limbs, people with terminal illnesses, war veterans, and teens in foster care, they all wanted to see this cow who was so full of joy despite his challenges. They needed to know that they were not alone. They needed inspiration. They laughed at his antics. They reached out to touch his red coat, to have him nuzzle their open palms, as if his resilience were contagious and they could take some of it home with them.

When Dudley was out in the pasture with the other animals, he was frisky and adventurous. They all played together and grazed side by side. When we had guests, hosted groups, or held open Sundays, the other animals would sometimes wander away. Dudley, though, would lie down in a meditative state, holding perfectly still and allowing guests to lean into him as long as they wanted.

In early spring 2016, we hosted a group of children in foster care. These kids had abused, neglected, and damaged pasts. They came from the absolute worst circumstances. Their therapists and caregivers brought them to the Gentle Barn hoping that the healing that happened there could help the kids do better in school, get along better with each other, and work through their own issues.

The second time these visitors came to the Gentle Barn, I invited them to spend some time brushing and hugging Dudley. When we got out to the pasture, Dudley was busy, playfully bonking heads with the other cows. They were having a really good time, and I didn't want to interrupt, but the children had looked forward to being close to Dudley and needed his attention. They looked disappointed that it might not happen.

I walked over to where Dudley was sparring with his pals, looked him in the eye, and said, "Dudley, I see that you're in the middle of something, but this group of kids really need you. Is there any way you could spare just ten minutes with them so they can brush and hug you, and then you can go back to playing?"

Dudley stopped to look at me, then swung his head to take in the group of children before looking back at me. The look in his eyes was a "Yes."

He walked away from his bovine friends toward the kids, lay down, and closed his eyes to indicate that he was ready. I brought the kids over to him, and they brushed, hugged, and kissed him. Once the last youngster had said goodbye and walked away, Dudley stood up and headed back to his play-mates. I looked at the clock on my phone and saw that it had been exactly ten minutes. He had come through whole-heartedly, giving exactly what was asked of him.

Once a month, Jay and I would travel to Tennessee to check in on the animals, train staff, and facilitate groups of children in foster care. During one of these visits, on a particularly warm and sunny morning, I headed to the pasture to meditate. Dudley loved hanging out under a giant hickory tree in the middle of his pasture, enjoying the shade and happily munch-ing on the nuts. That's where I found him on this lovely morning, resting on the ground, chewing his cud, and lazily swishing his tail side to side. The scene was so inviting that I picked a spot next to him to meditate.

As soon as I sat still and closed my eyes, flies buzzed around my head, landing on my face. I tried to focus only on my breathing, but I couldn't ignore the impulse to brush away the flies. Then there were the crawling bugs I had not antic-ipated. I'm sure I achieved only a few minutes with my eyes closed, but when I opened them to see Dudley's sweet face, it all seemed worth it. Afterward, Jay showed me a picture he had taken of Dudley and me, sitting together with our eyes closed, breathing in and out at the same time. Jay said, "You know that's Buddha, right?!"

Jay's words stayed with me. I believed Buddha's sweet spirit was the energy that had pulled me to Dudley, but was her *actual* spirit within him? I needed to know if Dudley was Buddha. I needed to find out if there was such a thing as reincarnation.

On our next flight to Tennessee, a few hours before we landed, I spoke to Dudley in my mind. I asked, if he was the reincarnation of Buddha, that he show me proof. I set the bar high, asking for something that no other cow since Buddha had provided me: I wanted Dudley to wrap me in his neck and hold me, the same as Buddha used to do.

We traveled the thirty minutes from the airport to the Gentle Barn, dropped our bags off at the house, and then quickly drove across the street and up the hill to the barn. As I got out of the car I could see Dudley standing near the gate ex-pectantly, his big, beautiful eyes staring right at me, teddy bear ears alert. I walked over to him, wrapped my arms around him, lowered my face down onto his shoulder, closed my eyes, and waited. Then Dudley wrapped his neck around me and held me for about twenty minutes! My arms tightened around him, tears sprang from my eyes, and I could hardly breathe, frozen in his magical Buddha embrace. I believed in reincarnation on that day, in those twenty minutes. Buddha was back with me as Dudley.

That night after dinner, I sank into the couch, kicking off my shoes and curling my legs under me. I pulled the plush throw over my lap and savored the time to contemplate what my experience with Dudley meant to me. Perhaps our animals and our loved ones come back to us more often than we realize? As much as we choose them, maybe they have chosen us as well. Maybe there's a more significant reason our animals are with us? I've always known they love us, and we love them, but what if they also came to heal us, to help us fulfill our destinies and our purpose? What if there are far more angels and guides around us than we even realize? Would we feel less alone if we knew that was true? Maybe I'm here doing my work, and I'm surrounded by angels and guides that I can't even see, being pulled forward by forces I don't even realize?

As I mused, certain mysteries from my life began to make more sense. After all, how did I get inspired to dream of the Gentle Barn as a seven-year-old? How did it seem so inevitable, an idea I could never leave behind or outgrow?

I thought about the prior year. Why did I choose to rescue a cow as my birthday gift? How was Dudley that cow? How did I know that a second Gentle Barn would be possible or sustainable? How was it that people around the world were falling in love with Dudley and cheering him on?

There are many things in our universe we will never fully understand until we ourselves transition. But one thing was for sure, my Buddha had returned to me, and I wasn't going to waste one more minute denying it!

The first part of what the woman on the end of my bed told me that frosty December night had become a reality. Now I couldn't help but ruminate on why she had said that it would become the "best two years" of my life. I couldn't stop myself from feeling concerned: Why specifically two years? Was the Gentle Barn going to close down in two years? Would there be a disaster that destroyed our property? Would something happen to Jay and me? Why had she said only two years?

Two years after opening the Gentle Barn in Tennessee, I found out why.

Dudley had developed a sore on the bottom of his residual limb. It was small and harmless at first, but we couldn't get it to heal. We had many vet visits and used multiple treatments, ointments, and salves. Nothing made it go away. Ronnie consoled me with the information that this was very common with amputees, human and nonhuman alike. He told me that sometimes skin grafts are needed, and that he himself had gotten several over the years. Dudley's veterinarian also assured us that it was no big deal. After several more weeks of trying everything we could think of, to no avail, our veterinarian recommended that we take him to UT Knoxville for a skin graft.

The procedure was very successful. Doctors said that once the swelling went down, Dudley would be able to walk using his prosthetic as before and resume his life at the Gentle Barn. Twenty-four hours later, however, Dudley was still not himself. He didn't have his usual energy, wouldn't take his favorite cookies, and wasn't cuddling. I knew something else was wrong, but the doctors kept reassuring us that it was normal for some animals to take longer to recover, acclimate, and get their appetite back. The day after his surgery, we all held steady. The second day, we started to feel more concerned but tried to stay positive. By the third day, even the doctors looked worried. And by the fourth day after his skin graft surgery, the doctors told us that they needed to take Dudley back in for exploratory surgery to figure out why he wasn't recovering as expected. Jay and I were freaking out!

All the color was drained from my face and tears threatened to spill over as I sat across from Dudley, waiting for them to take him to surgery. Dudley was looking directly at me, continuously, not taking his eyes off mine. He had never stared at me with such intensity before, and my stomach began to feel jittery as my anxiousness increased. It all gave me a bad feeling, like he was trying to tell me something. Even when I tried to push it away as only nerves, my intuition told me that this surgery would be different from all of Dudley's prior medical treatments.

When the doctors arrived to take him into surgery, Dudley looked at me, then Jay, then our staff, then around to all the nurses and doctors, not leaving any person out, as if he was saying, "Farewell and thanks." My brain still hoped for a positive outcome — I think I even prayed — but my heart felt heavy.

When the surgeon opened Dudley up, they discovered a hole in his stomach caused by the anesthesia. The surgeon came and told us the news, that Dudley would not survive because of the damage and asked us permission to help him out of his body. The update was like a shocking slap across the face. We were rendered almost catatonic. How could we have come this far only to lose him now? How could all of his determination to heal himself and others come to such a pointless end? Why was this happening? I couldn't fathom how Dudley could go from our joy-filled healing cow, world-renowned and bathed in the light of his public's love, to taking his final breath on a metal surgeon's table, under the harsh glare of fluorescent lighting.

I could feel myself tremble, as if my muscles were dissolving under the harsh new reality of losing Dudley, similar to what happened right after letting Buddha go. I wasn't sure I could fight the urge to collapse to the hospital floor and wail, but as soon as my knees started to buckle, I heard a voice in my ear saying, "Don't you dare! I have not left you. I will never leave you. I am right here and always will be!"

I felt Dudley next to me, as if he were wrapping me in his soft neck, holding me up, giving me strength. Tears still ran down my face, unremittingly, for hours, but it was different this time. It was clear to me that Dudley was present in an undeniable way.

Dudley passed away exactly two years after the woman appeared on my bed. It indeed was the best two years of my life because he brought understanding, hope, and happiness to countless people worldwide, and I got to be with my Buddha again!

Dudley's surgeon, doctors, and nurses were also badly shaken at the outcome. The mark Dudley made at that hospital, the way that he expanded their hearts to the intelligence of cows, was profound. Most of their clients were from the beef and dairy industry, and their main job was to fix cows to be well enough to be sold to slaughter. I witnessed hospital staff treat other cows very aggressively to get them to do what was needed. When we first brought Dudley to the hospital, we talked to the orderlies, nurses, and doctors and made it very clear that Dudley was not to be treated that way. We explained that his purpose was to heal people, and that he always had to be treated gently. Instead of pushing him around to move him forward or backward or to get him to do something for his treatments, we coaxed him with cookies or peppermint candies. He would do what we asked with no force needed. Through Dudley we were able to teach others how to move cows gently, kindly, and slowly instead of with the negative motivation of pain. Because of Dudley, the hospital employees now thought of cows in a different way, and Dudley's memory lives on there to this day. Dudley did as much good work inside that hospital as he did at the Gentle Barn.

We always had memorial services for our animals who pass away, but they had always been for staff and volunteers. Because Dudley was world famous and meant so much to so many, we decided to make his memorial service public. We sent out the word, and the response was overwhelming. Hundreds of people wanted to travel to attend in person, and Jay and I had to scramble to find a place that would work. The largest venue we could find in Knoxville would accommodate five hundred people, and we would live stream the service to everyone else worldwide.

On the drive to Dudley's memorial service, street signs that read *Dudley* kept popping up. Then for an entire mile there was a truck that drove beside us with the word *Dudley* written on its side in huge letters. We drove past a park called Dudley and Horton's Park. Dudley was everywhere that day.

The venue was filled to standing room only with people who loved Dudley. We had thousands on the live stream. Many of us stood at the microphone to tell stories about him and the impact he had on our lives. Some brought us flowers or gifts, others brought photographs, and everyone brought stories of how Dudley had made a difference in their lives. Thousands of handwritten and emailed messages were sent in from people around the globe, describing what Dudley meant to them.

One woman's email told how she had been suicidal and had planned how and where she was going to end her life. In what would have been her final days, she happened upon some Dudley videos through social media and watched them. Seeing what he had gone through and his will to find joy again gave her the courage to know that she could go on too. I later got to meet this woman in person, and we shed tears together about how Dudley helped save her life.

Another letter came from a woman who suffered agoraphobia and for a decade had not left the confines of her house. She too watched Dudley's videos and followed his story, through them realizing that if he could be brave, she could too. Because of Dudley, she dared to leave her house and went to enroll as a volunteer at a sanctuary in Canada, where she lived.

Dudley also inspired people to make concrete changes in their lives. One man, who had visited the Gentle Barn reluctantly with his wife, hunted as a hobby. When he met Dudley, he began to sob into his shoulder, apologizing for all the suffering he had caused other animals and promising Dudley that he would change. I heard later that this man was living a vegan lifestyle.

To this day, I am stopped in airports by people who fell in love with Dudley, followed his story, were shattered when he died, and remember him fondly. Social media posts and emailed stories still arrive weekly with personal memories of Dudley. Millions remember where they were and what they were doing when they saw the news that Dudley had passed away. A judge in a city courtroom wrote to tell me that she learned about Dudley's passing during a trial. When she glanced at her phone and saw the news that Dudley had died, she had to excuse herself from the courtroom to go and cry in her chambers.

When I think about Dudley, I can picture him ripping the Halloween decorations off the barn wall and running around the property with them in his mouth, Jay playfully chasing him, while the rest of us watched and laughed so hard we cried. I think about how he would lie down at exactly ten o'clock every Sunday morning, when guests started arriving to visit him, not getting up until two in the afternoon, when visiting hours were through. My senses still remember the way it felt to have Dudley's neck encircling me in his hugs, my face resting on his side. I can almost feel my nose being tickled by his fuzzy fur.

After opening our first Gentle Barn, in California, our dream was to have a location in the biggest city of each state so we could get as many people as possible to understand how wonderful animals are, to heal those who are hurting, and to open the most hearts. In Tennessee, we had rented the property in Knoxville so Dudley could be close to his surgeon. After Dudley transitioned, we decided that more people would know the Gentle Barn if it were in Nashville. Jay went ahead of me to look for a property while I held the fort in California. Once Jay narrowed down the search to three favorites, based on location, acreage, amenities, and cost, I went to Nashville to choose the finalist.

The first property was huge and had a great big log house that looked like a hotel. It was gorgeous! But the energy on the land was dark, and I did not feel at peace there. When we arrived at the second property, I got out of the car at the top of the hill, closed my eyes, and breathed in deeply. I knew right away that it was the one. "But Ellie," Jay exclaimed, "you didn't even see the barns or the house!"

"Close your eyes, Jay," I answered back. "How does it feel?" We both shared a moment of silence as we took the land in, not with our eyes or brains, but with our hearts and intuition. After a few silent moments we turned to each other with tears in our eyes and agreed, this property was our sanctuary. It felt just like Dudley! We could feel him all around us, in the radiant sunshine, the green pastures, the spacious barns, and especially under the old hickory tree right in the middle of the cow pasture. We were home!

Today the Gentle Barn Tennessee is home to dozens of animals, including Dudley's Destiny. On the front side of our cow barn is a life-size mural of Dudley. Every animal is rescued, every person is healed, and every heart is opened in memory of our Dudley, his endless joy, and his giant cow hugs!

I continued to meditate with Buddha/Dudley and feel her presence with me when I closed my eyes. I would hear her say she was still with me and would always be with me, but I wanted proof. I told her that if that was true, I needed something to happen that would make me believe without a shadow of a doubt.

In the fall of that year, a few months after Dudley passed, I was driving down Vasquez Canyon, a windy road in Santa Clarita just round the corner from our California Gentle Barn location. With hills on the right and gorgeous canyons on the left, it's like a small-scale Grand Canyon. The layers of rock are red, orange, and yellow with deep crevices visible, except in the winter, when the green grasses grow tall. The road usually has very little traffic, so it's easy for my imagination to take me back to when the Tataviam tribe lived here, probably familiar with these very nature-made rock caves, gathering water in these same creeks along the bottom of the ravine. As I was slowly driving, enjoying the view, about a million white butterflies suddenly rose up from the side and crossed the road in front of my car, like a floating cloud. I pulled myself out of my daydream, screeched my brakes to a hard stop, and waited a long time for the butterflies to cross the road. I checked to see if there were cars behind me, if anyone else was seeing this, but I had the road to myself.

This was a first for me. I have often seen small clusters of butterflies around a plant or dancing on the breeze, but a group of thousands all heading the same direction? The rest of the week I asked everyone who lived in our area if they had seen the enormous cluster of butterflies, sure that it would have made the news, but I could not find a single story or a single person who saw them. I wondered, was that my sign from Buddha/Dudley?

The butterflies were impressive and otherworldly, but sometimes unusual things happen in nature. Maybe, like the monarchs, they were migrating. I persisted in asking Buddha/Dudley for one more sign, some other proof that I couldn't deny. Nothing happened for a few weeks, and my vigilance in looking for a sign started to fade.

Then one night, I was tucking Cheyanne into bed. My phone battery had run down, so I turned the phone off and plugged it into an outlet in the bathroom. I lay next to Cheyanne, singing some sleepy-time songs, our arms entwined in a delicious mom-daughter cuddle. I could feel her body relax and get heavy as her eyelids began to close. Suddenly, there was a very loud sound outside her bedroom door. Hoping it was just something my other kids or my husband was watching on TV, I ignored it, hoping it would stop. It did not stop. I called out to the rest of the family for help, but no one answered. The noise seemed to be getting louder, and with Cheyanne now fully awake, I went to see what was going on. To my shock, it was my phone, playing our YouTube videos of Dudley, one after the other! I had not been watching YouTube at all previously that day, and I had never arranged the Dudley videos in this fashion. Cheyanne crawled out of bed to see what was happening, and we both watched in awe. Once my phone finished playing every Dudley video ever uploaded, it went to black, switching itself off.

"OK," I said out loud, with a laugh. "Message received. I will never doubt again that you are *really* always with me!"

I had heard other people talk about signs from their loved ones and had read books about it. This was the first time I had experienced signs myself! I had almost dismissed the huge group of butterflies right in front of my car, seen only by me, as coincidental. I wondered, how many signs sent from our loved ones go unnoticed or ignored? I decided I would pay more attention moving forward and accept more things as messages and signs from angels around me. Sunsets, rainbows, cardinals, butterflies, hummingbirds, shiny coins, and written signs could all be love notes from loved ones crossed over. I was going to make sure that I never missed them again!

CHAPTER FOUR

MAYBELLE

There is a song inside each of us.
Never stop singing until you are heard.

— MAYBELLE

Dudley had given the Gentle Barn a huge leap forward in public awareness both nationally and internationally. As much as our presence had grown, my ability to trust my own intuition had also grown much stronger, thanks to Dudley. As our Nashville location grew in popularity, we received calls every week about animals who needed rescuing, many of them with nowhere else to go. What had started as an occasional request turned into dozens every week.

I knew I had to trust my intuition about which animals could be helped most at the Gentle Barn. I would often have a strong feeling, like the animal was connecting to me before we even heard about them. For a couple of weeks in 2017, I could feel a connection to a specific dairy cow; I could see her already in my mind's eye. I knew, somehow, that we were going to find one another, and she would become part of our family.

My staff, hearing me predict the arrival of this dairy cow, would say things like, "Hey, I looked on Craigslist and there's a dairy cow." And I would say, "No, that's not her." And then someone else on staff would say, "I found this auction house with a lot of dairy cows. Do you want me to go and check it out?" And I would answer, "No, she's not there. I know this doesn't make a lot of sense, but I'm connected to her already. I can feel her. I know her in my soul. She's on her way, and I'll know when it's her."

My staff would nod and accept what I was saying, even though they had never experienced someone with my process, one I didn't understand fully myself. I appreciated that they trusted me, and together we waited for my intuition to be confirmed.

I finally got the call about Maybelle. "She belongs to a farm family and has been their source of dairy for over eight years. They said they need to retire her now."

Dairy cows are generally "retired" when they are older and can't have any more babies. "Retiring a cow" is the euphemism used for sending them to slaughter. But Maybelle had been so good to this family that none of them had the heart to have her retired in that manner. But they couldn't afford to keep and feed her without a purpose. The family formed a prayer circle, hoping for a miracle: that they would find somewhere safe where she could live out the rest of her life. When I got that call, I knew she was the cow I had been waiting for.

The minute I saw Maybelle's face — with her big, bright, gorgeous deep brown eyes; her alert, fuzzy black ears; her petite, swirly, black and white body; her seahorse-shaped nose — I fell in love with her and recognized her as the soul I had been feeling for the past few months. I explained to her who I was, where we would take her, and what her life would be like. I pictured images in my mind of the animals she would live with and all the wonderful people who would care for her, stroke her with gentle hands, and give her the freshest, most nutritious food and clean water. I asked permission to bring her home, and she easily hopped up into the trailer.

Maybelle's stall at the Gentle Barn was already set up with organic hay, fresh water, and clean, soft bedding. After settling into her bedroom, she began to moo incessantly. At first, we thought she might be nervous or want to go outside. She had to stay in her stall until the veterinarian examined her, but even after the vet saw her and proclaimed her healthy and we moved her out to the pasture for the day, she kept on mooing. Maybelle paced back and forth and walked around the perimeter of the property, calling out as she went. When she saw me, she would walk over to me and moo in my face. It was clear she was trying to tell me something. I remembered back to when Karma did the exact same thing and knew there was only one reason that cows behaved like this: they are calling for a baby. I ran to find Jay and told him that Maybelle had a baby somewhere.

Everyone connected to Maybelle's prior family insisted that there was no calf. I had to believe Maybelle, though, in the same way I had trusted Karma, so I asked Jay to drive back to the farm and drop in, without an appointment, to look around for a baby.

When Jay arrived at the farm, sure enough, there was a small black and white calf tethered on a chain, standing all alone. Jay found the farmer and asked if the calf belonged to Maybelle. The farmer said, yes, that was her baby, but he was weaned quite a while ago and they had not shared a pasture in many months. He didn't think that Maybelle would still be attached to him. They were raising the young cow to be used as meat for the next year. Jay explained that Maybelle was apparently still very attached to him and was in great distress.

The farmer tried to convince Jay that having the baby wouldn't solve the problem and maybe she needed to be milked. But Jay pressed on, asking if we could reunite the son with his mother. Finally, the farmer agreed to let us have the baby as well if it would make our family happy.

Jay loaded the baby into the trailer, and once he was on the road headed home, he called me and told me the good news. I was in the pasture with Maybelle when he called, and through sobs of relief, I told her that her son was on his way. Maybelle planted herself on top of the hill that overlooked the road and stared down the street until, forty-five minutes later, she saw our little red trailer chugging up the hill. She began mooing frantically and raced to the front gate. The son, in the trailer, heard his momma's cries and started mooing back. The two of them were calling frantically to each other, back and forth, while Jay backed up the trailer and aligned it with the gate to the cow pasture. We opened the back doors to the trailer, and out ran Maybelle's beautiful little boy, racing excitedly to his mom. Maybelle licked him all over until he was soaking wet, and then they scampered off together. They have been inseparable ever since. We never milked Maybelle, and her son never nursed since he was already weaned. It was very clear that Maybelle was crying because she wanted her son, and for no other reason.

Maybelle and her son, who we named Miles, settled into our bovine family nicely. They became instant friends with the other cows, grazed in the pasture, lay down to meditate daily, and separated from the others each evening so that Maybelle could give Miles a good bedtime bath and put him quietly to bed. In the colder months we would bring all the cows inside at night to sleep in the barn, and in the summer months the cow family would stay out in the warm pasture all night and sleep under a bright blanket of stars.

Soon after Maybelle and Miles arrived, a foster agency reached out. They had heard about the healing work going on at the Gentle Barn and wondered if they could bring a group of children in the foster care system to our Tennessee location. We were told that these children had unimaginable background stories of severe neglect, physical and sexual abuse, abandonment, constant relocation, and rejection and failure in their school settings. Overall, these were high-risk children.

We agreed and set up a program to run from September through June. The children would come to the Gentle Barn for the first time in September, and then return once a month thereafter. On their first visit, the kids gathered around the picnic tables so we could talk about a few things before going out to find the animals in their pastures. Everyone was really excited to be there, except one eight-year-old who I will call Adrianna. She wouldn't look at me, speak to me, or sit down with us. I didn't force the issue and let her stand off to the side. I spoke to the rest of the kids but talked loud enough for her to hear me.

I told them that the animals they were about to meet had been rescued from sadness, loneliness, and fear, knowing full well that these kids had experienced the exact same conditions. Some of the animals came from a situation where they had no food, others had no home, and still others hadn't known what love was.

I could see in the kids' faces that they were listening intently, except Adrianna, who was going out of her way to show me that she wasn't interested in anything I had to say. She turned away from me, arms folded across her chest defensively, and kicked at the ground in impatience.

As with every group of children who visit the Gentle Barn, I asked them to take turns sharing a word that described who they were and then to say what their dreams were for their life. It's important to me to help our guests cultivate self-awareness and hope for the future because I think we are each born knowing who we are and why we've come to be here. We lose this inner knowing through the various trials of life. As soon as we go to school, we're told to sit down, be quiet, follow the rules, and trust someone else instead of ourselves. We lose our individuality. We forget who we are. We forget why we've come. As grown-ups, we bury ourselves in jobs that are safe but unrewarding, in relationships that are unfulfilling, and we suppress our natural intuition and instincts in an effort to fit in and to please others. Eventually we forget our dreams because we no longer recognize the person we once were.

Each child took a turn describing themselves, with words

like *smart*, *strong*, and *nice*. They shared their dreams, which included becoming a teacher, a veterinarian, a firefighter, a police officer. Adrianna refused to answer, and I didn't insist. I needed her to know that however she showed up, however she was feeling, was OK with me.

When we were done, we went to see the cows. The kids held brushes and took turns grooming the cows. They scratched the cows' backs with their fingers and giggled when one of the cows licked them back. On the way out of the cow pasture, they all, one by one, put their arms around the cows, their faces down on the cows' sides, closed their eyes, and took a few breaths, clearing their minds. I could see them letting their troubles fade away, the weight of the world lifted off their shoulders for a while.

Adrianna stayed with the group but refused to brush a cow or even step into the cow pasture. We spent the rest of the day hugging chickens, cuddling turkeys, and playing with goats. Everyone participated except for Adrianna, who barely took her gaze off the ground.

On the way back to their cars, we stopped at the wishing well, where I explained how the Gentle Barn had been my dream since I was seven years old. I told them I didn't finish college, I didn't have a lot of money, I was not popular in school and did not have a lot of friends; there was no reason my dream came true other than I just refused to give it up. I told the group that they were also here to live their dreams, and if they refused to give up, eventually they would also come true. We all formed a circle around the well, put our hands on the magic wishing well rocks, closed our eyes, made silent wishes to ourselves, and then clapped two times before stepping away. The kids' faces were beaming, their eyes shining, their heads held a bit higher as they each hugged me goodbye and skipped off to their rides.

Adrianna refused to come close to the wishing well and

remained sulking in the background. Her counselor tried to convince her to participate, but I stopped her.

I imagined that there was a very good reason why Adrianna did not want to participate and trusted I would get a chance to find out what it was if I didn't press too hard. I've learned to give children the same respect I show a newly rescued animal. When I come on too strong, both children and animals become more defensive and resistant to help. But if I just do my thing, come and go without paying any extra attention to them at all, eventually they come to me. It is then that I can begin to understand what they need most.

I wanted to say just one thing to Adrianna that would help her feel OK about her first visit. I didn't want her to feel she had let me or anyone else down. I went over to the van she was about to get into, purposely casting my gaze down to be less intimidating. I said to her, "You didn't participate today, and I want you to know that it is totally fine. You didn't brush the cows, hold the chickens, cuddle the turkeys, or answer my questions, and it's totally fine with me. But now I need you to look at me and listen for just thirty seconds."

Adrianna softly stepped away from the van door and looked at me for the very first time. I slowly raised my gaze to meet hers.

I said, "I'm thinking that you probably have really good reasons to be angry, sad, or frustrated. I just want you to know that I see you. I see how much pain you're in. And I want you to know that you can come back to the Gentle Barn next time, or you don't have to. Or you could come back and not participate. Or you could participate if you feel like it. You can show up however you need to, and it is completely fine with me."

Adrianna kept eye contact with me while I spoke to her. Afterward she got into the van and they drove away. I wasn't sure I would ever see her again. I wondered what had happened in her short life that shut her down so completely. What hell had she been through? I knew that the animals at the Gentle Barn could help her, and I hoped that she would give them a chance.

The next month came, cars arrived, doors flung open, kids came skipping down the driveway, and in the lead was Adrianna, who flung her arms around my waist and beamed up at me with a smile. I was thrilled to see her! I gathered them all up after our hellos and sat them all down on the picnic benches. Knowing that these children were sadly no stranger to broken homes and missing families, I told them about our brand-new cow, Maybelle. I told them about her crying and her reunion with Miles. I shared that Maybelle did not fully trust us yet and explained that we would have to move and speak softly and slowly to show her that she and her son were always safe. Everyone listened intently, including Adrianna, who looked into my face the whole time.

Afterward we went into the barn, everyone anxious to meet Maybelle. The kids all said hello, fed her cookies, and brushed her softly before moving on to see Dudley and the other cows. Just as we were about to leave the barn, I looked over my shoulder and saw Adrianna straggling behind. I watched as she bent down to the ground, took a handful of dirt in her little hand, stood up, and threw the dirt in Maybelle's face. Her counselor also saw this and rushed over, grabbed Adrianna by the wrist, and took her outside for a stern talking-to and then back to me for an apology. Luckily Adrianna's aim was worse than her anger, leaving Maybelle unfazed.

Without looking at me, Adrianna mumbled, "I'm sorry."

I said, "Adrianna, you don't have to be sorry."

This got her attention, and she looked up at me inquisitively.

"You don't have to be sorry. You probably have a million

good reasons why you're so angry. You are probably so angry that you could hurt or kill someone. I get it."

Tears immediately sprang to her eyes with this unexpected validation. I could see that buried deep behind them was pain, abandonment, and deep disappointment, covered up by a perfect smile maintained across her face, insisting on showing the world that she was in control.

I tossed and turned in my sleep that night, haunted by her smile. I wondered why she couldn't let the tears flow, refusing to be vulnerable. The next time the group came out, I pulled the counselor aside and asked her to tell me a little bit more about Adrianna, how she was doing, what her circumstances were, and what she'd been through. The counselor told me Adrianna had told a teacher she was being abused at home. Instead of reporting it, the teacher called her father into the office and told him what Adrianna had said. The father, of course, denied all claims and then brought Adrianna home that night and beat her within an inch of her life.

The counselor said Adrianna was now temporarily removed from the home and was living in foster care. Adrianna had refused to tell her therapist or counselor what really happened in that home. It was urgent that they find out, though, because her parents were fighting to regain custody, and if she didn't speak up, the judge would have no choice but to return Adrianna to her parents.

At the end of our session that day, Adrianna asked if she could stay a little longer and check out our gift shop. She disappeared behind shelves of T-shirts and toy cows, horses, and pigs. Moments later, she came running out with my first book, *My Gentle Barn: Creating a Sanctuary Where Animals Heal and Children Learn to Hope.*

And she asked, "You're Ellie?"

"Yeah."

"Is this you?"

I said, "Yeah, that's my book. That's my story."

She went silent for a minute and then asked, "What's it about?"

I said, "Well, it's about my childhood." She sat down on the floor in front of me and looked up at me, wanting to hear more.

I continued, "When I was a kid, there were some babysitters who touched me in my private places. It made me feel ashamed, and it made me feel scared. It affected the rest of my life, until I worked to heal from it." There was a pause while Adrianna digested this information. I felt vulnerable and exposed and wondered if I had shared too much.

Adrianna looked around to see who might be able to hear. When she confirmed that it was only the two of us, she said, "I was sexually molested too."

I knew this was important; the counselor would need Adrianna to reveal what had been happening to her at home. I was elated that she was confiding in me and had to work hard to control my voice, so I didn't come off too excited and scare her away.

"Really?" I said slowly. "Can you tell me more about it? What happened to you?"

Adrianna revealed things that we hear only in horror stories, things we don't want to believe actually happen to real people. She told of sexual and physical abuse that no child should know about, let alone go through. She let it all out, painting a picture of ongoing abuse, gross neglect, and betrayal from the very people she counted on most. This little eight-year-old had a life void of basic nurturing, care, or love. How had she survived it? I marveled at her resilience and strength. I'm sure my face went pale, as my breathing became very shallow, imagining the cruelty she had endured.

"Oh, my God, I'm so sorry Adrianna," was all I managed to say.

About an hour and a half later, when Adrianna and her counselor were leaving, the counselor turned to me and said, "You're the only person she's ever told any of her story to. If we can get her to talk about it in front of her therapist, then the therapist can report it to the judge, and we can keep Adrianna from ever having to go back to that home. Would you be willing to go to her next therapy session?"

"Of course!" I answered. I had a definite feeling that saving Adrianna might be one of the most important things I would ever do!

I waited until the car had backed out of the drive and was long down the street before I put my face in my hands and had a big, long cry, not only for Adrianna but for all innocents suffering at the hands of others, and for the strength of those spirits wanting to be witnessed, saved, and given a chance.

A few weeks later they arranged for me to go to Adrianna's therapy appointment. Thankfully, the same thing happened there that happened at the Gentle Barn. I started by telling a little bit of my story, and then Adrianna shared hers. This time the revealing conversation happened in front of the therapist, who could report it all to the judge.

Adrianna shared how in her family, she was never allowed to complain or express sadness or anger, that she always had to be perfect, with a smile on her face. She described the betrayal that she experienced after she reported the abuse to her teacher and said that after the final beating from her father, she decided she would never tell the truth or ask for help again. While sharing this background with us, she never broke her perfect smile, never shed a tear or even frowned. She was perfectly composed. Too composed.

The issue with Adrianna's high capacity to bury her real

feelings was that those emotions have to come out somehow. My concern was that by submerging her authentic feelings, she might begin to act out on smaller children or helpless animals. When I expressed my concerns to her counselor, I was told that she was already acting out sexually on younger children and had killed some small animals. If by eight years old she was already hurting small animals, it was only going to get worse from there. Her violence as an adult could be more severe, continuing the cycle of violence and suffering. We had to find a way to connect her with her feelings in order to save animals, other people, and ultimately, to save Adrianna!

At least step one was accomplished; she had told her story in front of her therapist so the judge could keep her out of her home. We praised her repeatedly for telling the truth. I went to multiple therapy sessions because Adrianna refused to open up there without me. In one of these sessions, Adrianna asked me what I did when I was angry. I told her that I went outside and screamed anything I wanted to say to the sky. The therapist told us that she had a field out back, behind the building.

I said, "You have a screaming field here?!"

With a smile on her face and a twinkle in her eye, the therapist said, "Yes. We do."

We both looked at Adrianna and said, "Let's go to the screaming field!"

This was serious business, connecting Adrianna to very painful feelings, but we tried to make it light so she would want to participate.

In the "screaming field," I explained to Adrianna that we can take all our feelings, thoughts, hurts, anger, sadness, and any words we had bottled up inside of us, and we can just scream them out. The sky would be our witness and could take our pain far away. We agreed that on the count of three, we would all scream as loud and long as we could.

We held hands and counted to three, and the therapist and I screamed as loud as we could. Adrianna stood silent, watching us with wide eyes but a closed mouth. She had probably never seen an adult express themselves in this way. I could tell she was fighting to keep her composure and control.

The therapist and I continued screaming, trying to thaw out her control, little by little. We screamed until all our breath was gone, then took a deep breath and screamed again. By the third time we screamed, Adrianna joined us, with a very soft, breathy yell. We kept encouraging her to scream louder, asking her what she would say if she could see her father and mother right now? What would she say to them?

For a moment, Adrianna's face got real — the corners of her mouth falling from their usual smiling pose and her eyes growing dark — and on the count of three she screamed with us. She screamed "I love you!" as loud and long as she could, with fists clenched, eyes closed, veins in her neck bulging, and spit flying from her mouth. That was the very first time I caught a glimpse of the real Adrianna, and she was breathtaking. The therapist and I threw our arms around her in a group hug and held her tight, allowing her to feel the safety and acceptance of expressing her true feelings for the first time.

The following month when Adrianna and the other kids from the foster agency came to the Gentle Barn, I wanted to encourage them to connect even more to their feelings about the many traumas they had experienced in their young lives. Jay and I laid big blue plastic bats out on the picnic table. "Today we're going to work on anger," I told the group. "You can put your anger into the bat and let it out by hitting the tables or the ground." Jay and I handed out a bat to each child. They seemed inhibited at first, but it didn't take much to get them started. Soon they all were screaming and swinging their bats at the table or the ground.

Although Adrianna had done so well in the last therapy session, in front of the other kids she had trouble connecting. While the other children smashed their bats, screamed as loud as they could, and fully embraced the exercise, Adrianna held back, her face frozen in a fake smile, as she laughed uncomfortably at the others.

When the other kids were done, bats bent and broken, faces tearstained and puffy, completely spent, Jay took them to the kitchen to have a snack. Adrianna moved to follow them, but I said to her, "Hey, you are not quite done. Come back."

When she returned, I gently explained to her, "Adrianna, this isn't a game. This isn't funny. Tragic, unfair, and cruel things happened to you. You were never safe to express your anger, sadness, or pain. All those feelings are trapped inside your body, and they're shaping your future. You are beautiful, brave, and strong, and you deserve to be happy."

I asked her, "What's the worst thing that's ever happened to you?"

"Being beaten."

"Was that fair?"

"No," she answered, and the smile disappeared from her face.

"Did you deserve that?"

"No."

"Did it hurt your body?"

"Yes."

"Did it make you bleed?"

"Yes."

"Did it make you scared?"

"Yes."

"Did you deserve to be loved, held, cuddled, and kept safe?"

Adrianna fell silent, pensive, and serious.

"How angry are you, Adrianna?" With a look of determination and focus, Adrianna walked over to the picnic table, picked up a bat, and beat the table until she had smashed the bat into pieces. She picked up a second and a third bat and did the same. Adrianna went through three bats, demolishing them, screaming "I hate you! Why weren't you my daddy? Why didn't you protect me? Why didn't you love me? Why did you do that to me? You were supposed to keep me safe! I love you! I love you! I hate you!"

When she was done, she had a red and swollen face from crying, a hoarse throat from screaming, and a body she couldn't even hold up anymore. She sank to the ground, no smile anywhere in sight. I softly lifted up her chin so her eyes could meet my gaze, and I told Adrianna that she looked real, soft, vulnerable, and beautiful.

I gave her a hug and told her she was a hero. She had been through things that could have easily broken anyone else. She told the truth, she expressed her anger, and she did it even though it hurt. Slowly a smile spread across her face. Not the fake smile from before, not the smile to please others, but a real, humble, sweet smile, the smile of a survivor. The smile of someone who's been through hell and back and finally found the strength and courage to face it, to talk about it, to feel it, and to get it out of her system so she could move forward.

When we are hurt, betrayed, abandoned, and abused, we develop coping mechanisms to survive it. Those only work so long, and then they come back to haunt us. When we can finally connect to our fears and traumas, face them head-on and look them right in the eye, we conquer them, overcome them, and in the process, we find our true selves. Every animal rescued at the Gentle Barn has experienced that moment when they set their past down and walked away from it. Now that Adrianna tasted the sweet victory of authenticity, I knew her life would be forever changed. She would no longer need to hurt others because her truth was out there for everyone to see.

By the end of our yearlong program, Adrianna was a real girl, with hurts, tears, anger, and pain. After graduating from our program, she was adopted into a new family. Like any of us on a healing journey, she still had more issues to deal with and battles to face, but she was now facing them with the truth as her shield and her real feelings as her sword.

Unbeknownst to us, Maybelle was pregnant when we brought her home, and on the eve of a blood moon, she gave birth to a baby girl we named Eclipse. After eight years of having her babies taken away and their breast milk stolen for people to drink, Maybelle was able to retire at the Gentle Barn with two children to love and nurture for the rest of her life. Maybelle became the matriarch of our bovine family and Tennessee mom to all of us, helping us heal hundreds of children like Adrianna, who came to us looking for hope.

CHAPTER FIVE

THE ST. LOUIS SIX

No one can stop you unless you agree with them.

— CHICO

More than 200 million turkeys are raised in the United States every year. We all know why.

One year, right before Thanksgiving, Jay and I were able to rescue Alice, Enid, Sun, Angel, and Adeline. Of course, they didn't have names where they had grown to young adulthood. They had known only despicable living conditions, waking up each morning to watch as, one by one, members of their group lost their lives for a holiday celebration.

We had heard about a backyard full of mistreated turkeys and the woman who was selling them to the neighbors. The customers would look over the group, pick the turkey they wanted, and the woman would process them right then and there. The day before Thanksgiving, there were five survivors. We drove to her place with a trailer to buy the remaining five, while Jay talked with her by phone, insisting that she leave them alive. They were filthy dirty and trembling in fear when they arrived at the Gentle Barn California.

With good food, clean water, and warm shelter, along with love and respect, they slowly began to trust that they wouldn't be harmed. In a few months' time, they began walking around the barnyard like a little posse, searching for tiny flowers to eat, chasing bugs, dust bathing in the sun, and experiencing Gentle Barn life together. Once they finally trusted us, they learned to cuddle. When any of us would sit on the ground and put one leg on either side of them, they would come closer and fall asleep in our laps while we petted them. Often guests were brought to unexpected tears once they witnessed the same love and affection in these birds as in their own dogs and cats at home.

About a year into their rehabilitation, Adeline, one of the Thanksgiving five, started getting extra-cuddly with us, following us around, and seeking out our undivided attention. She was the first of the turkeys to cuddle with us. As if jealous, the others all started picking on her. The close-knit girlfriends were becoming quite territorial and jealous of each other, constantly bickering and picking fights. It soon became clear that this girl gang needed some space from each other.

While we were trying to figure out what to do, Enid passed away from a heart attack in her sleep. Turkeys are genetically engineered to get very big, very fast so they can be slaughtered at only twelve weeks old, and by the time they are full grown they have respiratory issues and often their giant hearts give out. Genetically engineered turkeys are not designed to live a full life; they are set up to fail from day one.

We found a great adoptive home for Angel so she could establish her independence. Alice and Sun still got along very well, and we knew they could happily live together at the Gentle Barn. It occurred to me that our Tennessee location did not have a cuddle turkey. Since Adeline absolutely loved falling asleep in people's laps and being the center of attention, I thought she'd be a great fit there. She could still be the queen of turkey cuddling, and the move would end our turkey wars. Now, it was a matter of getting her from Southern California to the middle of Tennessee.

We took the opportunity for an all-girls cross-country road trip, with two female staff members; our daughter Cheyanne, who was ten years old at the time; our dog Socks; Adeline the turkey; and me. The human adults took turns driving, stopping for short breaks along the way, and Cheyanne sat in the back seat of our Toyota Highlander with Adeline and Socks. We cranked up the music, and as we were singing, Adeline chirped along. We passed around snacks, and Adeline happily gobbled up blueberries, grapes, and trail mix, and then lifted her head to look out the back window. It was so fun to see people drive by and do a double take when they realized there was a turkey in our car, checking them out.

Each evening we would announce on our social media and to our email list where we planned to stop for dinner, so any local folks who followed the Gentle Barn online could stop in and say hello. No matter the restaurant, we took Adeline in with us. We would gently pick her up, carry her out of the car, and set her on the ground, and she would walk with us from the parking lot to the restaurant. When we got to the restaurant, Adeline would walk right into the middle of the crowd and stand still as people pet her, cuddled with her, and took photos. She would stand motionless like a movie star until the last person walked away. Then the restaurant would bring her food and water, and Adeline would walk around, gobbling and squawking, to everyone's delight.

By the time Adeline was done greeting her fans, we would all be tired from our day of travel and ready to find a nearby motel for the night. We would walk into the front desk area all together: four humans, a dog, and a turkey. The person behind the desk would invariably begin to say, "Wait, you can't bring… Is that a turkey?"

The front desk person would start to laugh, bringing the other employees to meet Adeline and take selfies. As it turned out, no one minded having a turkey as an overnight guest.

We stopped at the Grand Canyon near Sedona and at the Civil Rights Museum in Memphis, and our little turkey drew more attention than the sights and displays. Not one restaurant, store, museum, or motel asked us to leave. We felt community, acceptance, love, and warmth at every stop. When I think about the best experiences of my life, this wonderful road trip and seeing the human-changing force of one twenty-pound cuddle turkey is close to the top.

As our band of girls trekked across the country, a news story about animals was capturing the nation's attention; six cows who were facing imminent death in a St. Louis slaughterhouse had escaped. The lead cow had somehow managed to bust out a section of the corrugated steel fence containing the herd inside the slaughterhouse. He then, by pure force of will, pushed through two other barriers. Five other cows, sensing this was their only chance at freedom, followed quickly, before the staff realized what had happened. As the cows ran for their lives, they crossed surrounding streets and parking lots, looking for open land, and people began uploading videos of the escapees as they dodged between cars. Soon, as the news caught wind of the story, helicopters were buzzing overhead, first local news and then national. Meanwhile police and other authorities tried to round up the cows into a corner where they could be captured. St. Louis residents took to the street, cheering on the lead cow with chants of "Chico! Chico! Chico!" Being in an industrial district, however, the cows had no way to escape, and one by one, all six were cornered and caught, loaded into trailers, and returned to the slaughterhouse.

Within an hour, people started calling the slaughterhouse, requesting that they let the cows live. Most callers put a gentle pressure on the owner to give the cows the chance at life they had fought so hard to win, but some people even threatened the owner if he didn't. A small group of animal lovers set up a GoFundMe account and raised the money to buy and save the cows. The slaughterhouse owner agreed to release them to a sanctuary if one would agree to come and get them.

Four days went by, and no Midwest or even East Coast sanctuary came to get the cows. By the fourth day, the owner of the slaughterhouse was impatient and announced that he was going to process the cows in the morning. That's when our phones started ringing.

We are known for taking animals that no one else will take. Our donors, supporters, and followers all over the country started calling us after hearing the news, begging us to save the lives of these cows. "Can you do anything? Can you save them?" Even former St. Louis Blues hockey star David Backes and his wife Kelly called to see if we could help the cows.

As a rule, Jay and I don't pay slaughterhouse owners for animals, as that is basically putting money into the same industry we want to abolish. We never want to financially support the meat industry. At the same time, the money was already raised and would go to waste if not spent on saving the cows. The owner was willing to release them. For both Jay and I, the thought of standing on principle when we knew these six cows would die was unendurable. People around the world were hoping they would be saved. We knew that the cows' survival would also be a great way to get out a strong message about why we must move more rapidly to share the planet more equitably with animals. This news story had already made millions aware of how cows, like humans, had the will to survive, the courage to try, and even unique features and personalities.

Since I was on the road trip to Tennessee, Jay boarded a red-eye flight to Missouri, arriving in the morning in time to stop the slaughter. He transported the cows to the hospital, where they were treated for infections, parasites, and wounds. Afterward, Jay found a forty-acre foster home right across the street from the hospital that was willing to take the cows, which gave us the time to gather our thoughts about how we could best support our new cows and what steps to take next.

Meanwhile Adeline was delivered, safe and sound, into the care of our staff at the Gentle Barn Tennessee. We had been close from the beginning; whenever she saw me, she would run to me and then follow my every move. The road trip had bonded us even more, and when the time came to drive back to California, it took everything in my power to tear myself away from her. I gave her a long, teary-eyed goodbye cuddle before getting in the car to go home.

With tears streaming down my face, I said to my travel companions, "If only the world could experience Adeline's friendship, cuddling, intelligence, and companionship, there would be no way anyone would eat turkeys anymore." As we drove away, I was comforted by the idea that our superstar Adeline would be opening hearts in Tennessee for the rest of her life. And she did step happily into her new role as "best cuddle turkey" in Tennessee, and every Sunday long lines of people would wait their turns to take her into their arms.

Meanwhile "the St. Louis Six," as our brave group of bovines were affectionately called, spent the fresh spring days at their foster home, sloshing around in the giant pond, grazing on sweet grass, and lying in the shade of hundred-year-old trees. All six were boy cows: two black ones, two red ones, one blond one with a white face, and one black one with white, marbled sideburns.

Like turkeys, cows are genetically engineered to grow very big, very fast so they can be slaughtered, usually right after their first birthday. Even though each cow already weighed about a thousand pounds and was still growing, they still had sweet, innocent baby faces. If they had been left naturally with their mothers, they would still be nursing. They were very young to have already experienced such tremendous fear and betrayal.

Day after day Jay and I would sit at a table, with paper and pen, trying to figure out where our famous St. Louis Six could live. We didn't have room at our Tennessee location and did not want to put them through the four-day drive to our California location after going through so much trauma already. I searched through the emails and offers we had received about the cows but found that the farms on offer were a long way from Missouri. I felt tremendous pressure and responsibility in having to decide where the cows would go for the rest of their lives.

While Jay and I contemplated our options, we got some bad news about one of the six, who had been injured during his capture and roundup back to the slaughterhouse. His leg became swollen, causing a significant limp. We took him to the hospital, where they could not conclusively determine what was wrong but managed to stabilize his leg for a while. A couple of weeks later his leg got worse, and he was rushed back to the hospital for more treatments and tests. By the time they were finally able to diagnose him with a blood infection and fractured leg, it was too late. His leg was the size of a tree trunk, and he could no longer walk and was in excruciating pain. The veterinarian, out of treatment options, advised that the kindest thing to do was to help him out of his body. Jay held him at the end, giving him the name Spirit. As Spirit's soul left, Jay offered him what were undoubtedly the first and only gentle strokes he had ever received.

It was time for me to meet the cows. I thought that by meeting them, I could get a sense of what they wanted and needed and be better able to find them a forever home. After a long flight, Jay and I rented a car and drove the three hours to the cows'

foster home. When we parked the car, I got out and walked to the three-rail wooden pasture fence. The five boys were lined up in a row about a hundred and fifty feet away, looking at me. Chico, the cow who had led them all to freedom, walked slowly toward me. The others hung back, watching Chico's every move. When he got close to where I stood, I could feel a powerful energy radiating from him. He locked his eyes on mine, and the wisdom streaming from him to me was so palpable that I found myself on my knees, hanging on to the bottom rail of the fence, still looking at Chico. Tears spilled from my eyes, and I could not speak. I felt the impulse to bow at Chico's feet, but there were other people around and I didn't want to freak them out.

When I composed myself, I looked over my shoulder at Jay and said, "They have come with a story to share with the world, and we've got to help them."

Chico then turned and walked slowly back to join the others, and they resumed their day of grazing and exploring.

I returned to Los Angeles while Jay stayed in Missouri to find a realtor. Together they searched for properties that might be turned into a place for the St. Louis Six. (Even though there were only five of them now, we kept the name St. Louis Six in memory of Spirit.) A couple weeks and many different properties later, Jay called to let me know he had found a gorgeous property that he wanted me to see. He could see its potential as our possible third Gentle Barn location.

We drove up a long driveway that curved around a grove of trees. When the driveway straightened out, I caught my breath. Before me I saw an expansive green lawn, a log house, and two large barns. Butterflies filled my stomach as I stepped out of the car, already imagining the barns filled with rescued animals. The bigger barn had an enormous covered arena where animals could stay dry and sheltered during the harsh Missouri winters. The smaller barn had individual stalls where we could house chickens, goats, sheep, and pigs. Jay and I walked together, down the sloping property, to a long stretch of grassy pasture and another small barn. Dense woods edged the pasture behind the barn. I could already envision the St. Louis Six calling this spot home, grazing on the grass, resting in the small barn, and scratching their sides against the trees, munching on fallen leaves and enjoying the shade.

The last area we visited was the house on the property, which had bedrooms where my family or visiting donors could come and stay, as well as an apartment downstairs for the resident on-site staff. There was a big living room and a warm kitchen, where I could already imagine shared meals and laughter at the end of long days.

My heart beat faster in excitement as I realized the place even had a pond! I wanted to pull off my socks and shoes and wade around in the muddy banks to find frogs and tadpoles, like I had when I was a child. This was becoming a true full circle moment in my life! I thought about how my dream of having a big place, full of animals, had been conceived right here in St. Louis. And now, here I was decades later, back in Missouri, a place where we would now establish our third Gentle Barn!

I had to suppress a joyful yell of "We'll take it!" to the realtor, who was touring the property with us. I couldn't wait for Jay and I to get back in our car, so I could find out if he was feeling the same way. Sure enough, we both agreed the property would make an excellent spot for the Gentle Barn Missouri. Now there was the question of how to fund a project of this size. We started a GoFundMe campaign and, thanks to our generous donors, raised the money to purchase this dream location in just three weeks.

Once escrow closed, the real work began.

The first thing we had to do was put proper fencing around

the pasture for the cows. Each day Jay and I woke at the break of dawn. Together with community members who wanted to help, we put up fencing until we were covered in sweat and bugbites, with bleeding fingers and backs that ached. We would stop only for a quick lunch break and then get back to work. We scrubbed what would become the pig and smaller animal barnyard fencing with soap and warm water. Once the mossy green stains were gone, we reinforced the fencing with wire mesh and dug a narrow trench around the perimeter to put several feet of wire fencing into the ground below, so predators could not dig under it. We predator-proofed the bird rooms by putting mesh wire on the floor, roof, and all four walls. We even built a snack shop and store, working until 2 a.m. most nights, no doubt earning our hot showers before collapsing into bed for a brief four hours of sleep.

After the fencing and building were complete, we added beds of shavings or straw to all the stalls, hung bags full of hay, installed big water buckets to every room and pasture, put in fans and heaters, and added roosts for the birds. We stacked the feed room with bales of hay and straw and lined the wall with large metal cans full of chicken feed, oats for the goats and sheep, pelleted pig food, grain for horses and cows, and sealed containers of bedtime cookies for everyone. Now all we needed were animals!

Animals start their recovery process not when they arrive at the Gentle Barn but the moment they step up onto the trailer. When we pick up animals it is essential that they're not rushed, forced, or coerced onto that trailer but rather given the time they need to go on peacefully. Taking the extra time to speak to them, explain what is happening and why, and build the trust they need to jump onto the trailer by themselves creates a bond that will help them trust us and settle in once they are home.

We had not yet purchased a truck for the new farm, so we

hired a hauler to drive the St. Louis Six home. I then prepared the cows for the transfer. Through mental images, I showed them what our new property looked like. I visualized for them the sweet green grass that would be under their feet, the canopy of trees overhead, the peaceful shelter of the barn, and the respectful kindness from our staff, volunteers, and future guests. I promised them they would be happy and remain together for the rest of their lives. Then I asked Chico for his trust and cooperation in stepping up into the trailer so the others could follow. Chico contemplated his options for a few seconds. He was still distrustful of humans, so this was a big ask. He looked at my face and I returned his gaze reassuringly and held my breath, and then he stepped up into the trailer. The other boys hopped in after him.

Jay and I drove alongside the trailer in our rented car and watched the boys on the drive. They all faced the same direction, with their noses out the windows like puppy dogs. They seemed relaxed, fully trusting, and looking forward to arriving at their forever home.

When we reached the Gentle Barn, backed the trailer up to the pasture gate, and opened its doors, the boys saw exactly what I had shown them through mental images — barn, pasture, fences, trees — and they hopped off the trailer like they had been there before, with no fear or hesitation. Our awaiting volunteers applauded gleefully as the cows started grazing, some of them helping themselves to big sips of water, as if they had lived there forever. The St. Louis Six were home!

It was Chico who had pushed through three fences at the slaughterhouse and led his brothers to freedom. It was Chico who'd led the escape through the streets of St. Louis, even charging toward the police and animal control officers, causing them to retreat a bit, so his brothers could run past. The boys trusted Chico completely and did as he asked. I knew that to gain their trust, I had to have Chico's first. Helping them forgive and let go of their pasts had to start with Chico.

Every day for months, I sat in the cows' pasture for hours to meditate, sing, and read out loud to them. At first, they were alarmed by my presence and would stand in a huddle by themselves. No matter what they were doing, they were always watching me. I felt like some kind of weird stalker.

I would leave them a pile of cookies when I left for the day, and the next day they would be eaten. Eventually they started getting used to my presence and stopped watching me so intently. They even turned their backs to me and lay down. By the second month, they started looking forward to the cookies and asking for them when I arrived. I would move slowly to avoid scaring them, place the cookies on the ground, and back up. Once I was a few feet away, the cows would rush forward, gobble up the cookies, and ask for more. I knew that soon they would be eating cookies out of my hands.

Even though the St. Louis Six were now happy to see me coming, Chico still jumped at any sudden movement and seemed to look through me instead of at me. I wanted to help him let go of his experiences at the slaughterhouse and move forward. I started a meditation practice to help him forgive, where I closed my eyes and visualized a thick cord of golden energy running from Chico to the slaughterhouse. In my mind, I took a giant pair of scissors and cut that cord, cutting the connection between Chico and the slaughterhouse forever and sending all the energy back to his body, making him whole and complete. I repeated that exercise every day until, four days later, Chico stepped forward and licked a cookie out of my hand, signaling that the forgiveness exercise had worked, and he had let his past go.

Eventually I was able to pet the boys' faces while feeding them cookies, which led to petting their bodies, which in time led to brushing and hugging them. Before we knew it, staff, volunteers, and I could sit down in the pasture, and the cows would lie down next to us, put their heads in our laps, and cuddle with us. In a matter of months, the St. Louis Six had successfully become part of our family.

Our societies and cultural systems have become very good at disconnecting a Thanksgiving roast, hamburgers at the drive-through, or ribs on the grill from the animals they come from. One reason is that most of what it takes to bring packaged meat to the refrigerated cases in a grocery store is done far away from our sight and awareness. We don't associate what we're eating with a living, breathing animal, with the same personalities and vigor for life as the dog we throw the ball for when we get home from work, or the cat who cuddles in our lap. Often we decide that the animals we love and can call *pets* — our cats, dogs, parakeets, horses, and hamsters — are different from the animals we eat. Somehow the animals we love are intelligent, affectionate, and worthy of protection, while the animals we eat are unintelligent and unaffectionate, would never choose to have a relationship with us, and are not worthy of a good life.

The plight of the St. Louis Six was for many people eye-opening, illustrating the fact that cows aren't mindless and un-feeling. The truth is, behind every piece of meat is an innocent and terrified animal, who if given a chance would be lovable once they felt safe.

At our new Gentle Barn Missouri, we also saved some chickens going to slaughter because they were too old to lay eggs, four pigs who were treated badly and raised only for meat, a group of turkeys who, after being abandoned in the wild, practically followed us home, and two scared and neglected donkeys who had nowhere else to go. We hired staff to care for them, organized volunteers to be their docents, and opened our doors to the public on Sundays and for private tours and field trips during the week.

One day we were told about a renegade sheep, living a feral life on twenty acres of abandoned land down the road from the Gentle Barn Missouri. He seemed determined to stay far away from human hands, as the police, animal control, and other rescuers and animal lovers had tried for over three years to capture him. Somehow, he outsmarted them all. Once we had officially opened our doors, the community started calling us about the feral sheep, asking if maybe we could help.

It was the dead of winter, with a few feet of snow on the frozen ground and nothing to eat out there but fallen leaves. The trees were barren, and there was no water source. The sheep's nails were wildly overgrown, and his coat was matted, hanging in long, dirty dreadlocks, covered in sticks and brambles. This was not a good life for anyone.

Instead of trying to chase and catch him as those in the past had done, I instructed my staff to set up a feeding station. Each morning at eight we would bring a bucket full of warm water, flakes of fresh green hay, and a bowl of sweet grain to the exact same place on the abandoned property. Then we would leave it there for the sheep to eat. When we returned the following morning, we always found the bucket and bowls empty and the hay eaten, surrounded by adorable sheep footprints in the snow.

After several weeks, the sheep came to look forward to our arrival and even ate while we were still there, as long as we were at least twenty feet away from him. While he happily munched on the food and warmed himself with the water, we started to set up a fence around him, adding a section each day, slowly and methodically.

Seven days later the fence was complete, and we only needed to close the gate with our illustrious sheep in the middle. As he tried to find a way out, Nick, our wonderful animal caretaker, caught him in a big bear hug.

We loaded the sheep in the back of Nick's Jeep, and I sat with him to hold him still as we drove to the Gentle Barn. I was sure he was terrified and felt betrayed, which was hard; I never want any animal to feel cornered. But I knew that in a few minutes he would see that our warm barn, with fresh food, clean water, and friends, was a much healthier and happier way to live. I hoped that this momentary betrayal would soon transform into trust and gratitude.

Because of the sheep's wild white hair and the intelligence that helped him survive and outsmart people for years, he was named Einstein. He settled in, and with time, patience, and the help of energy healing, kind staff, and the friendship of our other animals, he began to trust us.

Einstein soon became a fan favorite, delighting guests with his woolly coat, golden eyes, and inspirational story. At the end of his life, he became immobile, losing the strength of his hind end. I was awestruck watching Einstein, once so scared and resistant, receive massage therapy, acupuncture treatments, chiropractic adjustments, and hand-feeding from our staff. He had recovered so completely that he emitted gratitude and joy while receiving our care. Einstein took his very last breath while I held his head and stroked his face, surrounded by Jay and our loving staff and volunteers.

Hundreds of thousands of people visit the Gentle Barn each year, looking for hope, and this brings the Gentle Barn's mission full circle. We rescue animals who are broken and lost, with nowhere else to go. We help them learn to love, trust, and forgive. Then the animals interact with people who are trying to learn the same. It is as if the animals want to pay it forward once they are healed.

One of the visitors to the St. Louis Six was a young woman who had been terribly abused for years. She came to the Gentle Barn through an agency that was trying to help her create a normal life. It was Chico who wrapped his neck around her in a healing embrace. It was Chico who held still as she cried onto his shoulder. It was Chico who gave her strength and hope. And it was Chico who helped heal her heart and encourage her to keep going on her journey of self-discovery.

Once a month we hosted a group of people who lived at a homeless shelter. These city folk held chickens, cuddled turkeys, petted goats and sheep, and always ended their sessions by hugging cows. Intimidated at first, they warmed up in a matter of minutes, rested their weary faces on the cows' shoulders, closed their eyes, set their worries down, and received unconditional love and hugs from beings who knew all too well what they were going through.

Like the St. Louis Six and Einstein, these young men and women knew what it was like to run for their lives with nowhere to go. They knew what it was like to feel scared, lonely, hopeless, and defeated. They knew what it felt like to be desperate for help and yet feel invisible. And like the cows and our sheep, these resilient soldiers are not only running from their pasts but toward bright, shiny futures, where they too can heal, forgive, trust, and take the lessons from their pain and pay it forward to help others.

Before we say farewell to each guest, they are asked to write a wish on a rock and drop it into our wishing well. It serves as a reminder of who they are and the dreams they are running toward. If we know only what we do *not* want, we can keep running forever. If we know what we *do* want, then we can create it and make sure we get there. My staff and I tell visitors that until the end of time, wherever they are, whatever they are doing, and wherever they end up, their dreams are held safe and sound at the Gentle Barn. When they find themselves lost, they can remember their dream written in our well and run toward it. They always have huge smiles on their bright and hopeful faces as they hug us goodbye.

From Chico and his brave brothers, a powerful life lesson was sent to millions of news viewers and social media followers around the world: that we each have to take a bold chance to get ourselves out of an experience that is bad for us. We might be afraid to break away from others and out into the unknown, but staying will only result in our demise — even if it's not a physical death, we will die spiritually. We don't have to have all the answers about our future; we need only the first steps of courage to save ourselves.

Knowing what we do not want gives us all a better idea of what we do want. It is through bad relationships that we design our dream partnerships. It is from being in bad working conditions that we create our dream jobs. It is from suffering that we develop empathy for others. It is from experiencing challenges that we come up with solutions. If cows inside a slaughterhouse can dream of life at a sanctuary and attain it, then anything is possible!

Dare to run toward the life you want.

CHAPTER SIX

BUTTERCUP

No matter how much pain we're in, we can summon
the courage to be wise, brave, and full of Grace
when someone else needs us.

— BUTTERCUP

Certain animals and people seem to walk through this world as Zen masters, no matter what circumstances or experiences they are going through. Most of our rescued animals arrive with their guard up high, ready to flee in the opposite direction of any human that appears. It often takes weeks, months, and sometimes years for them to trust they are safe. But there are certain animals who instantly appreciate their new lives and enter wholeheartedly, as if they know they have entered the promised land. My very first cow, Buddha, was like that. And so was our beautiful rescued Jersey cow, Buttercup.

Buttercup was one of many animals we rescued as part of a California animal cruelty case we investigated for four years. The man responsible for the crimes was finally arrested and sent to prison, and all his animals were confiscated and brought to us.

Compared to the huge black and white Holstein dairy cows, the Jerseys used for dairy are quite small. They are golden-brown, with beautiful shiny black noses and chocolate-brown eyes you can drown in if you stare into them for too long.

From the moment I looked into Buttercup's eyes, I fell head over heels in love with her. She exuded grace and femininity, and unlike the other animals who came in from this cruelty case, she wasn't afraid of people. She ate, walked, and rested with a slow, self-composed manner that made everyone around her calmer too. Buttercup made us all feel like everything was going to be OK.

Buttercup knew how to be mothering, through and through. Often, when I found her lying down, I would lie down next to her and put my arms around her, rest my face against her shoulder, and close my eyes, and the thoughts in my mind would vanish. My body would melt into hers, my heart rate would slow down, and my breathing would find the same rhythm as Buttercup's. I found myself seeking out those comforting embraces, not only when I was having a hard time but also when life was great. I would seek out those embraces just because they felt so good. They were like a warm bath in the winter or a cool glass of water on a hot day. And they were always available.

Dairy cows are kept pregnant, for financial gain, as often and for as many years as possible. Whenever one is brought home to the Gentle Barn, there is always a good chance that she will give birth in the near future. When Buttercup arrived, her body was bone thin, except for her very round belly. We could count each rib. Her hips jutted out sharply, and her legs were long and spindly. Her belly made me think she was pregnant, and I worried about her health because of all the neglect she had endured. We tried making up for it by giving her the freshest organic hay, the cleanest filtered water, Sun Chlorella, and nutrient-rich grain, all to help her gain weight and boost her immune system. I spent time each day hugging her, singing to her, and telling her how much she was loved.

Three months later, on an icy cold winter night, our suspicions were confirmed when Buttercup went into labor. Jay and I woke up the kids, and we all went down to the pasture wearing thick coats, winter hats, and gloves and carrying sleeping bags and blankets to keep ourselves warm while we stayed with her until her baby was born.

Once again, Buttercup was completely Zen and calmly went through labor, as she probably had many times in the past.

After an hour she was cleaning up her soaking wet baby, who lay on the ground. As she moved over his small body, she made sweet low moos, the sounds mom cows make only to their babies. Once he was completely cleaned off, Buttercup used her nose to urge the baby to stand up and nurse. He seemed much smaller and weaker than other newborn calves, lying on the ground with his long, thin legs splayed out to both sides, his head wobbly and shaky. Buttercup nuzzled him firmly, moving him to get on his front knees and then use his back hooves to push himself to standing, but he toppled over, again and again. I began to worry that he wasn't going to survive since Buttercup had been so severely malnourished during the early part of her pregnancy.

After a couple of hours, knowing the baby needed nourishment, Jay and I held him in a standing position and brought him over to nurse from his mom, who seemed grateful for the assistance. We supported the baby's hips and shoulders until he was able to drink his fill, then brought him to rest in front of Buttercup and let him slowly slump back down to the ground for his very first nap. As the sun came up, our worries rose as well for this little boy who couldn't yet stand or walk on his own. When our veterinary clinic finally opened at nine o'clock, we called for them to come out and examine our new baby.

Once the veterinary team arrived and everyone was finished oohing and aahing over the calf's cuteness, they examined him. Buttercup watched but didn't interfere. I was grateful that she trusted us. Our vet reported that the baby's heart sounded strong. His lungs sounded OK. They then confirmed what I had been thinking: without proper prenatal care, calves can be born smaller, weaker, and with underdeveloped lungs. They encouraged us to continue monitoring him and assisting him to nurse every two hours.

Thank goodness we had saved Buttercup when we did and

she had given birth at the Gentle Barn, where we had staff and volunteers to keep her calf alive. We all took turns watching him in four-hour shifts throughout the day and night, to help him stand up, build muscle, and nurse. It took a week for him to be able to stand and walk on his own. In two weeks, he was running back and forth across the yard, playing, bucking, and leaping. At about the three-week mark, our veterinarians declared him "out of the woods," and we all breathed out a big sigh of relief. With Buttercup's permission, we named him Halo.

Buttercup was so nurturing and loving to all of us humans that it was no surprise that she was an excellent mom to her own son. She would give him soaking wet tongue baths and was constantly talking to him with those sweet little mother cow moos. She stayed by his side or attentively kept an eye on him as he ran around. Everyone in the cow family took turns playing with him, bonking heads and running around with him. They were thoughtful and gentle with him, even when Halo got really frisky and jumped on their backs. The other cows didn't get angry or scold this new family member. They helped to raise him as though he were their own.

Seven months later, the land for miles around Gentle Barn was ravaged by uncontainable brush fires. This is always a possibility in the California high desert, as the grasses and bushes get dry and brittle during the low-precipitation spring and summer season. The Gentle Barn was spared from the fire itself, but the smoke, soot, and falling ash turned the air almost unbreathable. Charcoal flakes from the fire floated down on the barnyard and house, covering it all like snow that became inches deep. Our staff members wore bandannas and scarves over their mouths and noses, and we tried to keep both animals and humans indoors as much as possible. We set up giant fans in the barns, trying to blow the air clean. When we were finally free of the smoke, dust, and falling ash and the wind had shifted, blowing most of it away from us, all the animals seemed to have fared well. Everyone went back to regular life, except for Halo. What started as a little cough from smoke inhalation turned into convulsions with racking coughs. With each passing day, his condition got worse.

Our veterinarians reminded us that Halo was bound to be more susceptible to the bad air quality because he had come into the world with underdeveloped lungs. We brought Halo and Buttercup into our infirmary. Lined with tongue and groove wood walls, the room was fully insulated, with clean, air-conditioned air, providing a much more sterile environment. We were hoping that in this room Halo's lungs could heal and recover. Unfortunately, over the ensuing weeks Halo continued to get worse. Even though he was getting daily vet visits and medications, his condition soon turned into pneumonia.

I worked round the clock with our veterinarians, fed Halo nutritional supplements, and brought in other energy healers and Reiki masters to help. I talked to people at many other sanctuaries, as well as veterinarians and other experts around the country, trying to figure out what else we could do. Every time I was with him, I would look him in the eyes and say, "Halo, we're doing everything we can. We're going to get you through this. You're going to be all right."

Halo's message back to me was, "No, I'm not."

At this point in my life, I was still keeping my ability to hear and communicate with animals on the down-low. Though I used it almost every day to understand our rescued animals better and to know what they needed and wanted, I still feared rejection and ridicule from the public. The main issue was my lack of self-acceptance. My animals didn't pay attention to that concern; they still spoke to me, insisting that I be who I was meant to be.

Halo was communicating his truth to me, but I ignored his

prediction. I did not want to hear it. I needed him to stay alive. I had to hold out hope for all of us who loved Halo: Jay, the staff, and our volunteers. Most of all I couldn't imagine Buttercup losing her son after every other baby had been taken from her in her harsh previous life. This was supposed to be her chance to finally raise a child of her own. I had a bad feeling in the pit of my stomach, but I continued working round the clock to save Halo.

One day, a few weeks after the pneumonia had set in, I could no longer ignore what Halo had told me. His breathing was loud and raspy, he was spending way more time lying down than standing up, and his coughing and sputtering made it difficult for him to nurse. The veterinarians shook their heads slowly in sad defeat and declared that there was nothing more they could do. They allowed Buttercup one more night with Halo and planned to return in the morning to help him out of his body.

I spent the night in the infirmary, talking to Buttercup and gazing at Halo's perfect little golden body, an exact miniature of Buttercup's. He was lying down, his head hanging low because he didn't have the energy to hold it up. The room filled with the raspy sound of his breathing. I continued to sing, pray, and hope for some kind of miracle. I am not a religious person, but weary from exhaustion and desperation, I kept repeating, "God, please help our precious boy. Please don't let him suffer!"

As if in response, Buttercup walked slowly over to where Halo lay, reached her head down toward him, and started licking his neck and face. It was as if Buttercup were whispering in Halo's ear that it was OK to go. He rested his head on the ground and closed his eyes. His breathing grew very slow and quiet. Everything in me wanted to scream, panic, call the vet, and stop what I knew was happening but didn't want to accept. I wanted to shake Halo and beg him to keep trying, keep breathing. But instead, I sat in the straw bedding, unable to move or make a sound, and watched Buttercup fearlessly walk her son home. She was strong and selfless, nurturing and reassuring. She did not panic. She did not utter a sound or cry out at all. She licked him softly while he took his last breath.

Once it was clear that Halo had left his body, Buttercup laid down in the straw beside him, holding on to his spirit as long as she could. Buttercup and I stayed there on either side of Halo, looking at his sweet, peaceful, baby face. We remained together like that deep into the night.

In the morning I put a halter on Buttercup and led her out of the infirmary, through the barnyard, down the hill, and back down to the cow pasture. I did not want her to be there when they picked up her son's body for burial. Buttercup had remained completely composed, poised, and grounded in her Zen-like nature until we reached the pasture. As soon as I closed the gate behind her, she began to bellow with every breath she took. Buttercup wasn't crying because she didn't know where Halo was. She wasn't calling out because she didn't understand what had happened. She was crying because once she had walked him home, done her job, and set him free, she got to focus on her own feelings, her own emotions, and grieve over the loss of the precious physical relationship they had shared that was no longer.

Buttercup immersed herself in a wailing grief for several weeks. I was familiar with her cries, as not much time had passed since the same sound came from me after bidding farewell to my Buddha, and then Dudley.

None of us tried to stop her. Instead, we joined her, sat with her, listened to her, cried with her, and held space for her while she mourned. The other cows encircled her while they meditated and chewed their cud, taking turns being with her during mealtimes. We took turns sitting with her, softly singing to her or playing soft music from our phones. Buttercup wailed and mooed until there was nothing left.

What I learned from watching Buttercup care for her son during his passage from his body was so profound that it changed me to my core. Buttercup taught me that when we help an animal out of their body, it's not about how we feel or how their death is affecting us. It's only and always about the one transitioning. There will be time for us to express our feelings once the animal has passed.

Buttercup taught me that when a loved one is transitioning, my job is to be quiet and reassuring, strong and brave, to hold them, love them, and allow their transition to be magical. I witnessed Buttercup nurture and love her baby when he came into this world, and she nurtured him on his way out in the exact same calm, collected, and supportive way.

Buttercup's lesson forever shaped the future of animal care at the Gentle Barn. I teach her way to handle death to every volunteer and animal care staff member to this day.

Some births into this world take many hours, even days. Some are quick and easy. The births out of this body are also different every time. Some pass after a long illness, some after a tragic accident. Some pass away in their sleep. No matter if the transition happens easily or with difficulty, the same things are important in those moments: quiet, peacefulness, and the company of those most important to us. It needs to be sacred. Whether we are helping someone birth into form or out of form, our job is to make it full of love and comfort, concentrating only on them, like Buttercup did for Halo.

When our animals pass away slowly and painfully, after a long illness, the experience is harder for the animal but easier for us as it gives us plenty of time to prepare. It gives us time to cuddle with them, thank them for their service here, and share how much we love them: a slow and sweet goodbye. When a loved one passes away quickly or unexpectedly, the experience is much easier for the animal but much harder for us. Even when someone passes in a shocking way, I honor Buttercup's teaching and am reassuring, calming, steady, and focused on them only. I know I can have my own feelings once they are transitioned and laid to rest.

About six months before the time Buttercup lost her son, six calves who were being fed only to become veal ended up coming to live at the Gentle Barn California. This was a result of the connections Jay has been able to establish over the years with owners of stockyards, auction houses, and slaughterhouses. He always approaches them without judgment, with a levelheaded professionalism, and the results have been brilliant. When one of them has animals that can't be sold or used because they are too sick, they call Jay to take them off their hands. Jay is always prepared to go in a moment's notice, keeping a large trailer hooked to his truck.

So it was that Jay received a phone call to come right away if he wanted to rescue these six veal calves. They were very sick and would soon be put down if they couldn't come to the Gentle Barn. Sadly, we lost one of the babies on his first day with us, and then it took almost seven months to convince the others to live. The calves made a complete recovery around the time Halo passed away. I realized that we had a mother missing her baby, and five babies needing a mom. Maybe they could help each other?!

Though the calves were black and white Holsteins designed to get very big and Buttercup was a petite Jersey cow, they took to each other immediately and bonded like family. Buttercup still had milk from nursing Halo, and she was happy to donate it to the five orphans. Buttercup groomed and bathed the calves each evening before bed, disciplined them when they became teenagers, and raised them until they towered over her and outweighed her by thousands of pounds. We had named the babies Star, Courage, Faith, Crystal, and Forgiveness. When we called them by name, they would all move toward us, like a black-and-white cloud, with a small yellow moon in their midst.

After losing her son, Buttercup could have easily shut down and stopped loving others or enjoying life. Instead, she gave what she had left over from her son to those who needed her the most. Instead of slamming the door to her heart shut, Buttercup kept her heart wide open. She took her pain and paid it forward. For the rest of her life, Buttercup loved her adopted children completely.

Years later, when Buttercup's five "babies" were weaned and stood over seven feet tall, she continued to stay close to them, coming with them to the feeder to eat breakfast as a family every day. One morning, as usual, we brushed her and kissed her pretty face, which was always full of sunny enthusiasm. We were about to put on her fly mask, which protected her from flies and the sun's glare, when, without warning, she dropped to her knees, rolled onto her side, and after a few shudders and exhales, passed away. In a matter of seconds, our Buttercup was gone.

Like all great Zen masters, Buttercup took her leave without drama, fuss, illness, or misery. She woke up to a beautiful day, ate a delicious breakfast, received our affection one last time, looked around, and simply bid this world farewell. I was in shock at how quickly she went and felt a deep pang, knowing how much I would miss her, yet simultaneously smiled as my heart confirmed for me: "This was a perfect exit for a perfect matriarch."

During my childhood, my grandmother and grandfather lived in South Africa, and whenever they came to the States they would bring me hand-carved figurines of elephants, which I set up and displayed with affection. After years of visits from my grandparents, I had hundreds of elephant figurines.

At the Gentle Barn when I hosted groups of children from foster agencies, rehab centers, domestic violence shelters, and homeless shelters, among the visitors there would often be a child who was particularly struggling or who connected more deeply with our animals. Each time I had an extra special interaction with such a child, I would go into the house, pick out one of those little elephant figurines, and give it to them to slip into their pocket to take with them. It always made them smile. I have only a small handful of those elephants left after hosting groups of children for twenty-four years.

Eventually, my elderly grandmother fell ill. By the time I could be by her side, she was unconscious and had stopped eating days before. The only thing we could do was give her morphine and watch helplessly. Her tiny, thin frame lay motionless on the bed, barely making a lump under the sheets. As fluid filled her lungs, she struggled to take each breath and made gurgling sounds as she exhaled. It was awful to listen to her without being able to do anything for her. Unlike with our animals, there was no humane release for my grandmother and we could do nothing but wait.

I remembered what Buttercup had taught me about being present for the person passing away and not making it about my own sadness. So I sat and held my grandmother's hand for five days as she lingered. I allowed the time to be hers, with whatever process she was going through. I would sing and read calming passages out loud to her. I spoke to her about my best memories of her and all the love I felt for her over the years. I reassured her that it was fine for her to go. When she took her final breath, her hand was in mine. To this day, walking my grandmother home has been one of my highest honors.

I felt a deep gratitude for having known Buttercup. My self-confidence was in a state of no growth before she came to the Gentle Barn. I painfully struggled to understand my voice and appreciate and trust my instincts. Buttercup became my blueprint for how to be strong, brave, courageous, certain, grounded, and centered even in the hardest of moments.

Buttercup and the other cows were like trees with roots miles down into the ground. Even when the wind blew and the branches were shaking, the leaves were rattling, and the trunks were bending, the trees would never break because they were rooted so deeply. Our cows held steady, no matter what was happening, who was on the property, what noise was on the street, or who was passing away. I too wanted to stay calm and remain steady no matter what was happening around me, and I had the greatest teachers to show me how.

CHAPTER SEVEN

FERDINAND AND LUCY

You are braver than you think,
and more resilient than you know.

— LUCY

Observing any situation where an animal is treated like a possession, like property, or with any level of cruelty depletes me completely. I know it happens all day, every day around the world. But to witness it in person, or even in a You-Tube video, wreaks havoc with my nervous system and drains my spirit. I know I can't rescue every mistreated animal, so I keep my focus on what I can do to help the animals in my care.

My husband Jay understands this about me, which is why on this particular day, he was the one at the auction house to rescue a calf. Separated from their mothers, calves are almost always counted as worthless by those who are there to buy "livestock." Female cows are usually sold while pregnant so that they weigh more, as the auction price is always per pound. Oftentimes these helpless mothers give birth in this chaotic place, and there is usually no shortage of unwanted babies at the auction house.

Having to observe so much mistreatment of animals is very hard on Jay too, but he goes to the auction houses and slaughterhouses knowing that he can save at least one life. On this day, the life being saved would be fully sponsored and brought to national awareness by 20th Century Fox.

Jay and I share the same philosophy: any reason to save an animal's life is a good reason. So we had enthusiastically agreed to a proposal from the big movie producer-distributor. 20th Century Fox would soon be premiering its new animated movie *Ferdinand*, based on the classic 1936 book by Munro Leaf, *The Story of Ferdinand*, about a young bull who would rather smell the flowers than fight. The studio's idea was to sponsor the real-life rescue of a little bull, to be named Ferdinand, who would live at the Gentle Barn.

To publicize the movie release, they wanted all of the star voice-over actors, the director, the animators, and anyone else who worked on the movie to meet the real-life Ferdinand, be photographed with him, and then have their studio party at the Gentle Barn. This seemed like a great way to bring attention to the Gentle Barn and our larger mission to make the world a peaceful place for all living beings.

While I was setting up Ferdinand's nursery with bottles, milk replacer, nutritional supplements, high-calorie grain, soft bedding, and organic hay, Jay was in the stadium seating at the auction house, watching people bid on cows who were being prodded to run in a panicked circle in a small, enclosed area. As the auctioneer rapidly called out dollar amounts over the cows' plaintive mooing as they were torn from their families, Jay wanted to look away. But as heart-wrenching as it was to watch, he knew he was there for a purpose: to find and rescue Ferdinand.

After a few groups of cows had been bid on, Jay noticed a beautiful big black cow who had been channeled onto the auction floor, alone. She stood still at the edge of the floor, near the wall, not running or trying to find a way to escape like the others had. When the bidding was done, they tried to usher her out and toward the awaiting stock trailer headed to the slaughterhouse, but she refused to move, even when hit with a switch. After a minute or two, the reason she refused to move became clear as a tiny head peeked out from behind her. The people in the stadium gasped and pointed at the baby this mom cow was protecting.

The slaughterhouse that had just won the bid on her had

no interest in taking the baby, and finally an auction hand came in with an electric prod and forced the mother to move out through the gate, leaving the baby behind on the auction floor. At the sight of his mom vanishing, the baby became hysterical, calling out and racing back and forth.

Horrified, Jay ran out of the stadium and down to where the owner of the slaughterhouse was organizing transport for the cow. Forgetting why he was there and focusing only on the pain of this mom and baby, Jay asked the owner if he could take the mom and calf off his hands. The owner said that Jay could have the baby but not the mom. Jay offered to pay whatever it would take to have the mom as well, but the people who had purchased her refused to relinquish her.

Jay had found Ferdinand. Without any other option, Jay loaded the newly orphaned calf onto our trailer and drove him home to the Gentle Barn. Cheyanne, who was twelve that year, and I waited outside the nursery we had set up for Ferdinand and watched for Jay's truck. Even before we could see it, we could hear Ferdinand's bellowing cries echoing from the road and up through the hillsides. My hand instinctively reached for Cheyanne's, not being able to imagine my bond with her being broken and knowing that it happens to animals every day. Sorrow filled the air through Ferdinand's long, mournful cries.

Jay carried the calf from the back of the trailer and into the nursery area. I could see how beautiful he was, with a jet-black coat and big, dark eyes. He would not eat or drink, instead running in circles, calling out for his mom. He was frantic to find her. As much as I wanted to hold him in my arms and comfort him, he wouldn't let us near. In twenty-four years of rescuing animals from the darkest places on earth, this was one of the most horrific displays of cruelty and suffering we had ever seen!

Cheyanne and I knew that Ferdinand would not survive if left alone in his separation anxiety and sadness, and we decided to move into the nursery and stay by his side night and day. It was cold at night, so we slept in our warmest winter pajamas, sleeping bags, hats, and gloves, although we did not get much sleep. Every time Ferdinand cried out, we would answer back to him that we were so sorry for his loss. We cleaned up his poop, offered him food and water, and remained by his side.

After three days, Ferdinand stopped racing around bellowing and slumped to the ground in an exhausted heap. It seemed obvious that he was giving up. He finally allowed us to hold his head in our laps, while tears ran from his eyes.

Ferdinand was at a crossroads and needed to decide whether to live or die, eat or starve, fight or give up. I had been at this crossroads myself and knew that no amount of intervention was going to help someone survive unless they wanted to live. For hours each day I would kiss Ferdinand's face, stroke his soft neck, and close my eyes to communicate with him. In my mind, I painted the picture of the life he would live at the Gentle Barn. I sent him mental images of the yummy food he would eat, the fresh water he would drink, the friends he would make, the games he would play, and the gentle hands that would love him. I pictured him kicking up his heels behind him in joy, jumping into the air in elation, playing with toys, and racing strong on his young legs. I knew he was not ready for those things yet, but perhaps the possibility of those things would bring him hope, and hope would inspire him to live.

Much to our relief, Ferdinand chose to live and finally started eating. The rest of the week he spent exploring, and he started coming to us for affection. Within a few weeks he was playing with a giant bouncy ball, headbutting it around the stall. We turned it into a game, where we would gently roll the ball toward him and he would lower his head and give it a push back to us. Other staff and volunteers started helping out, taking four-hour shifts during the day and then sometimes overnight, so Cheyanne and I could take hot showers and rest in our own beds. Ferdinand started trusting us, and we became a village of caregivers who slowly resuscitated him back to life.

20th Century Fox had the film release party at the Gentle Barn. It was a magical, star-studded evening with food and press. Everyone was happy about meeting Ferdinand and having a photo with him.

Once Ferdinand's thirty-day quarantine was over and he was finally a happy, healthy boy, exactly how I had visualized it all, it was time for him to have the companionship of other animals. We started by bringing one of our goats into the nursery with Ferdinand, but the goat seemed intimidated by him. It seemed that Ferdinand needed the friendship of another cow, but I didn't want to turn him loose in the pasture yet, as he was still quite small. Because of his rough beginnings and separation from his mother, I wanted him to still have the warmth, safety, and gentleness of the nursery. Which of our cows could I bring to the nursery to stay with Ferdinand until he was a bit bigger and ready to move down to the cow pasture to be with all of them?

Buttercup would have been a perfect choice to nurture and adopt Ferdinand, and I missed her now more than ever. In thinking about the rest of our cows as a companion for Ferdinand, I concluded that some were too big, too scared, or too bossy, and some were bonded with others and could not be separated. I was so busy lamenting that it could not be Buttercup that I didn't see the perfect cow for Ferdinand right in front of me. Then, in the middle of the night, I was awakened by a singular thought: "Lucy would be perfect." I sat right up in bed and said out loud, "Yes, it's got to be Lucy."

Lucy, one of our senior cows, was a miniature Hereford, orange in color, with a white face, long eyelashes, fuzzy orange ears, and a sweet, orange, heart-shaped nose. She was nurturing, unassuming, humble, kind, and gentle. She was indeed perfect! I asked her if she'd be interested in coming up to the nursery and befriending an orphaned baby in need, and she told me she would be honored.

I put a halter on Lucy, and she walked steadily beside me out of the cow pasture, past the horse barn, and up the steep, rolling driveway to the top of the property, where Ferdinand's nursery was. When Lucy came through the gate and saw Ferdinand's face for the first time, she let out an excited moo in greeting. I unbuckled the halter and slid it off her sweet face, and Lucy went right over to Ferdinand and started licking him. It was instant friendship. From that day forward, Lucy and Ferdinand ate together, took long naps side by side, and meditated at the same time.

Lucy loved Ferdinand so deeply and adopted him so completely as her own that her body produced milk for him! The first time I watched him suckle, I thought that maybe he was just playing around down there for comfort. When he came up for air with a thick, bubbly milk mustache, I thought I was seeing things. But sure enough, Lucy began nursing Ferdinand three times a day, every day. Her udders swelled, and his gulping, swallowing sounds were unmistakable.

One evening I showed Lucy and Ferdinand's nursing to an audience of thousands on a live stream. We all watched in stunned silence as he slurped happily, and Lucy held still with a look of bliss on her face. The next day we received an email from a lactation consultant who had seen that live feed. She confirmed that with stimulation, mammals can produce milk for adopted babies and told us that she helps her human clients do the same for their adopted babies all the time.

Lucy nursed Ferdinand early in the morning as the sun was rising, at midday before their nap, and again in the evening as the sun was setting, just before she bathed him and put him to bed. Lucy wore the same contented, blissful expression on her face that I had worn on mine when I nursed my babies; the love and joy on her face were unmistakable.

Lucy and her officially adopted baby Ferdinand happily lived together in our little nursery for the next ten months. When Ferdinand was a year old, it was time to bring them both down to the cow pasture to live with the larger cow family. Lucy had done an outstanding job raising her adopted son, but he needed to play with other younger cows, and she needed the community of her cow family to help guide Ferdinand further along.

We chose a day for the move and placed the same red cotton halter on Lucy that she had worn the day she met Ferdinand. While petite Lucy walked with us slowly and carefully down the driveway and back toward the pasture, Ferdinand galloped freely, explored, and ran circles around us. We knew he would never leave her. Once she led him through the cow pasture gate, he was surrounded by all the other cows, who came over to smell him, lick him, and welcome him into their family.

For the next two years Ferdinand grew up in the cow pasture. He now had many friends to bonk heads and play with, but he continued to be the happiest right beside Lucy. She could have weaned him anytime she wanted to, but Lucy still nursed him three times a day and bathed him with her tongue before bed.

Eventually Lucy's age and the continuous milk production began to put some strain on her system. To support her, we gave her heaps of alfalfa hay, bowls of sweet grain, and weekly acupuncture, massage therapy, and energy healing. Our efforts helped Lucy maintain weight and mobility for a while so she could keep up with Ferdinand, but despite these efforts, we could see Lucy slowing down.

One morning I went on my usual sunrise walk around the

property to see how everybody was doing. I found Lucy lying down in the barn while everyone else, including Ferdinand, was standing at the feeders eating their breakfast. I hopped the fence and asked, "What's wrong, sweetheart? Why aren't you eating breakfast?"

She struggled to stand up and showed me that she could not. I called all my animal care staff at work that day to come and help, and after thirty minutes of us trying to get her up on her feet, it became clear that she was unable to stand.

In the same way that Jay and I believe any reason is a good reason to save an animal's life, any reason an animal gives us for wanting to stay alive is a good reason for helping to make that happen. I searched Lucy's eyes to find out what she wanted to do. Lucy looked in my eyes, telling me that she had fulfilled her purpose and felt complete and ready.

"But Lucy," I argued back, "Ferdinand needs you. You can't leave. He needs you."

"He is much stronger than you think and more resilient than you know," she told me, "Have faith in him. I am complete."

I wish I could say I listened to her wishes. I second-guessed both of us in my hope that she was only having a bad day. I should have honored her wishes, asked her for instructions, and let her go with grace and dignity. I did none of those things. I knew that the heartache of losing a mom for the second time would be crushing to Ferdinand, so I pressed forward with efforts to keep her with us.

We called the veterinarian out, tried anti-inflammatory medication and acupuncture. We tried again and again to lift her, roll her, and somehow get her onto her feet. We even put her into a water flotation tank to lift her up on her feet with water, but as soon as we drained the water hours later, she just slumped back down to the ground again.

At the end of the day, exhausted, drained, and soaking

wet from the water tank, Jay, I, and our staff started coming to terms with the fact that we might not be able to save her. I started listening to what Lucy had told me all along: she was complete.

While we dried Lucy off and covered her with blankets for the night, she looked at me with a pitying expression. I could almost hear her thinking, "I forgive you for what you put me through today, but please don't do it again tomorrow." I apologized to Lucy, but at the same time I knew I would have equally regretted not trying to save our girl and keep her with Ferdinand.

That night Jay and I hand-fed Lucy dinner and bedtime cookies. Afterward Ferdinand lay down next to her, and the other cows formed a circle around them both for their last night together as a family.

Just before morning feeding the next day, I went down to the cow pasture and found them all exactly as I had left them, together encircling Lucy, with Ferdinand by her side. When breakfast was served, everyone stood up and walked to the feeders to eat. Ferdinand hesitated for a moment, not wanting to leave her, but Lucy wagged her head at him, encouraging him to go eat with the others. By the time the veterinarian arrived, Ferdinand and the others were lying down just outside the barn digesting their breakfast, chewing their cud, and meditating in a circle, this time with Ferdinand in the middle. The family supported Ferdinand while the vet and I set Lucy free. She made no effort or struggle, but rather put her head in my lap, swallowed her last cookie, and transitioned easily, peacefully, and quickly.

Our beautiful, loving, Gentle Barn bovine family kept Ferdinand safely inside their circle for months afterward. They all ate by his side, groomed him with their sandpaper tongues, and witnessed his process of mourning for Lucy. Ferdinand absorbed their love, and with Lucy and his first mom forever in his heart, he healed and grew stronger, just as Lucy had always known he would.

What Lucy had communicated to me about Ferdinand before she passed is true not only for Ferdinand but for all of us. We are all stronger than we think and more resilient than we know. It is the most painful times that bring us the most strength, the most challenging experiences that bring us the most resilience. No matter what we go through, no matter how much we hurt, we can get through it. There's always resilience. There's always the next step. There's always the next day. There's always the next one who will love us. There is always the choice that we can make to fight, to live, and to keep trying.

By Ferdinand's third birthday, he was outgrowing our smaller cow pasture area and barn, where the cows who greet and heal our Gentle Barn guests live. He seemed restless and bored and was beginning to be disrespectful to some of the elder cows. Now that Lucy had transitioned, we thought that a visit to our much larger Healing Center, where about fifty other rescued cows live, might make Ferdinand happier. There was more land to explore, space to run farther, and more cows around his age. Like a young adult, Ferdinand was ready to move out and see life from a larger perspective.

On a Wednesday morning, Jay and I hooked up the truck and trailer and backed it up to the cow pasture's front gate. Forming pictures in my mind, I showed Ferdinand our Sun Chlorella Healing Center's huge barn, giant feeders, and white fences, and the other cows who lived there. I promised Ferdinand that we would stay with him until he decided if he liked it there or not, and if he didn't like it, we would bring him straight home to our main location.

He stepped up into the trailer as if he had understood every word, excited about this new adventure. He looked out the window as we drove the ten minutes up to the Healing

Center. Within moments of stepping out of the trailer upon our arrival, Ferdinand was engulfed by the other cows. Worried that he might feel overwhelmed, I moved toward him, but he shot me a look that said, "I'm all good, Mom." I needed to back off and let him do this on his own.

The youngsters head-bonked him playfully, introducing themselves. The matriarchs licked and sniffed him affectionately. When introductions were over, the cow herd moved off as a group, with Ferdinand right along with them. The youngsters took him to explore the barn and the far side of the pasture, and the elders formed a grooming circle in honor of their new guest. Jay and I waited patiently for Ferdinand to return and let us know if he wanted to stay or come home with us. But Ferdinand never returned. The extended family of cows enveloped him and took him away, and he became a natural part of them, as if he had been there his whole life.

We knew he would now learn how to become a humble, happy member of a larger community. He had friends his age to play with and strong elders to keep him in line and instill in him good manners. Our Sun Chlorella Healing Center animal care staff brushes him every morning and gives him bedtime cookies every night. He loves his life.

When I visit the cows at the Healing Center, I eventually catch Ferdinand's attention and he comes meandering over to me. He always stands along the fence so I can scratch his back, neck, and hips. He gives me his full and undivided attention for about twenty minutes. Once his massage is over and I've had time to tell him how much I love him and how proud I am of him, he slowly walks back over to his waiting friends and family, where he belongs — now strong in stature and participating fully in his community as an adult cow.

My wonderful Lucy taught me that my attempts to protect Ferdinand from the pain of her passing away was robbing him of the experience of growing from it. When we allow ourselves and our loved ones to go through heartache, we also acquire the ability to grow in wisdom and in strength of character. The biggest challenges of our lives give us the greatest gifts, and often our darkest moments bring us to our brightest triumphs.

CHAPTER EIGHT

SOCKS

Never change for anyone, ever.
Instead, gather around you those who can love you
for who you are.

— SOCKS

When Gentle Barn California first opened, our days were filled with nonstop chores and caretaking, from sunrise to long past sunset. Jay and I had no staff then, so we fed, watered, groomed, and cleaned the animals by ourselves. We repaired the fences, hauled the hay, and shoveled out the barns, all the while making sure our two young children, Jesse and Molli, were completely cared for in every way.

Then some clients from a nearby rehab facility who were getting sober volunteered to help with projects at the Gentle Barn as a mode of therapy. One of the men who arrived to help restore some of the land was a die-hard animal lover named Dale. He had successfully completed his drug rehab program and was looking for a place where he could be happy and stay clean and sober.

Jay and I liked Dale, who was full of energy, walked and talked quickly, and threw himself into the projects wholeheartedly, always on the go. After talking it over, Jay and I came up with a situation that could work out to be a win-win. We offered Dale the chance to live in the comfortable trailer next to our house in exchange for his daily help taking care of the animals. He could stay there as long as he stayed off drugs completely, as we have always had a zero-tolerance substance abuse policy. We put the safety of our children and the animals first. Dale was happy with the agreement and was relieved to have a safe place to live and people who cared about his success with staying sober.

Dale's birthday was coming up, and since he was in the

trailer by himself in the evenings, we thought it would be great to adopt a dog for him. We went to the animal shelter, hoping to find a dog with a lot of energy to keep up with Dale. The attendant smiled and led us to the back area, saying, "We have the perfect dog for you."

She pointed out a husky mix with chocolate-brown fur, white socks, white chest, pointy brown ears, green eyes, and a fluffy tail. She was curled up in a ball on the ground and barely looked up at us.

The attendant said, "This is your dog."

I looked down at this deflated little animal. She seemed sullen and depressed. I couldn't imagine her having energy. She didn't even stand up to meet us.

"She's beautiful," I said. "But we really need an active and playful dog."

The attendant nodded confidently and said, "Yes, this is your dog."

She went on to explain that the dog had been adopted and returned to the shelter three times. People wanted to adopt her because she was so beautiful, but no one could contain her once they took her home. She was so full of life and energy that she didn't fit into a "normal" home or routine. No fence was too high for her to jump over, and then she'd sprint off to explore the neighborhood. The people who had adopted her had reluctantly brought her back to the shelter, unable to deal with her energy level. The shelter attendant told us that the dog was depressed only because she had been brought back to the shelter so many times. She assured us that once she was at home with us, we would see that she had a lot of energy.

When we were introduced to her in the shelter's dog yard, she crawled underneath the chair Jay was sitting on and cowered with her tail between her legs. She looked miserable and in need of help. That did it. Whether she was hyper or not, it didn't matter now, because we were taking her home. We gave her the name Socks.

Sure enough, after a couple of weeks of being with Dale and accepting her new life at the Gentle Barn, Socks's depression lifted, and she blossomed into an energetic and extremely intelligent dog who ran around our five-acre property to her heart's content. We never put her within a fence and allowed her to have run of the grounds, even at night. She could be authentically herself.

Dale too seemed to enjoy life with us, having family around and a purpose. We took him to 12-step meetings and gave him our full support, but sadly, two years later, his disease caught up to him and he began using once more.

Even in his drugged-out state, Dale realized he had broken our agreement, and he began to pack up and leave without us having to ask. I was grateful that he took responsibility, as the idea of having to kick him out would have broken our hearts.

As Dale was loading his belongings into his car, Socks watched him closely. I put my hand gently on Dale's shoulder, looked him softly in the eyes, and said in the kindest voice possible, "Your journey is your own. You have every right to do what you want and go where you please. I wish you the very best! But with the uncertainty of where you'll end up, can you please leave Socks with us? She deserves better."

Dale and Socks had become good friends, and I didn't want to separate them, but taking a child or an animal down into the depths of drug addiction is just not fair. Dale had every right to choose his own path, but I had to protect Socks, who would never understand what was happening. Thank goodness Dale agreed with me and drove away alone as I held on to Socks, teary-eyed, reassuring her that it would be OK.

It wasn't until we moved her into our house and introduced

her to our other dogs that I realized the extent of Socks's intelligence and generosity. She was incredibly attentive and followed me around everywhere I went. When I was sad, she would lie close to me, lick my face, cuddle into me, and allow me to kiss her forehead. When I was focused on work, she waited patiently by my side. When I had time to play, she would pounce on a toy and bring it to me, or race around with a toothy, white smile as we chased each other. She was so much fun.

Socks knew that it was appropriate to scold our children if they bothered her when she was sleeping, but she would never growl at the kids who came to visit the Gentle Barn. She was with me for every group tour and field trip. Socks was the boss at home and would reprimand our other dogs, but out in public she was humble and submissive with all other animals. I could take her with me to dog parks and beaches and other people's houses, and she was always a perfect companion. We quickly formed a deep bond, and without a doubt, she became one of the best constant companions I could imagine.

Socks and I forged such a close bond that she became my companion dog everywhere I went: planes, trains, boats, and automobiles; cities, countryside, seas, and mountaintops. She was with me all day and all night for over a decade.

The first time she came on one of our family vacations, we were river rafting, and I didn't know how she would feel about being in moving water. I got in the inner tube raft first and called to Socks, who jumped in and sat on my lap. Off we went, splashing down the river. When we got to the end, I told Socks to abandon ship, and we both jumped off and swam for shore. Then we ran up the hill to do it all again. She loved it!

Socks knew me better than I knew myself. She knew when I was upset, and she knew how to calm me down. She knew when I was sad, and she knew how to lift me up. Aside from Jay, she was my best friend.

In 2019, Socks developed arthritis in her legs and lost her hearing. I thought it no longer seemed fair to walk her through huge airports and ask her to sit for long flights, so I let her stay home. She seemed ready for retirement and was happy to lounge with our pet sitter when I left and happy to see me when I returned. After a while, she became picky with food and started looking thinner than before. She had never been overweight but had always had muscular form. I knew she was getting older and wanted to make sure she was OK as she became thinner and frailer. So we took her to the vet for a checkup.

When her blood work and the other tests came back, they revealed that she had stomach cancer. Our whole family was devastated!

I couldn't imagine my life without Socks, but I knew I would honor her wishes in the same way she had fulfilled my every wish for more than a decade. I went into my bedroom and sat by myself to clear my thoughts. Then I communicated with Socks with an open mind, asking how she was feeling and what she wanted to do. I posed the questions in my mind and sat silently, waiting for her to answer me.

Socks told me, "I'm fine for now. I know my appetite has declined, but don't worry about that. I'll eat enough to stay alive. I'm going to give you another year. It will be a wonderful year. I'm going to train your next service dog and make sure you're all right."

And then she added, "I have a list of things that I would like to experience before I go. I'd like to give you my bucket list." I took out a pen and paper and began to take notes. Socks told me that she wanted to see what it was like to do some of the things she had never done before because she was always so well behaved: She had never gone to the bathroom in the house, had never ripped up or chewed on anything, including her own toys. She had never jumped on the counters or tried to get food that wasn't meant for her. I could place a dinner plate of food on the floor and leave the room, and she would not eat it.

Now, during the last year of her life, Socks wanted to experience those things. She wanted to rip a toy into a thousand pieces and watch me pick it up. She wanted to take food off the counter. She wanted to know what it was like to dig in the trash. She wanted to eat everything that I was eating. And she wanted to have a day at the beach. That was her bucket list. I wrote it all down and put it on my dresser so that I could look at it every day and find opportunities to grant her those wishes.

Socks took her bucket list very seriously. After more than a decade of carrying her toys around the house delicately, never scratching them or roughhousing with them, she started destroying them like other dogs. She ripped them to shreds. She looked so happy when she was doing it that I just laughed and cleaned it up when she was done. We got her a brand-new, and very expensive, soft, fluffy dog bed. Now that she was thinner and older, she was sleeping less on the bed and more on the floor, and we wanted to make sure she was sleeping on something luxurious and soft. Instead of enjoying the dog bed like I imagined she would, Socks destroyed it. She shook it, dragged it, and carried it around and left pieces all over the house. She had never done that before, and I was happy for her. It took Jay and me three hours to clean it up, but it was worth it, knowing that she was able to check another item off her bucket list.

Socks started stealing food off the counter just like she told me she would. And she started barking at me every time she saw me eating, as if saying "Hello! You promised you'd share with me." She had never urinated in the house before, but now she peed in each room of the house. She did it only once in each room, then was satisfied.

While the spring of 2020 brought loss, sorrow, and change

to millions because of the Covid-19 pandemic, for me personally, it provided the unexpected gift of more time with Socks.
When I would have otherwise been traveling or working, I was
granted long hours to pay attention to her, like I had never been
able to before.

Since the Gentle Barn was closed for tours and the airline
travel restrictions kept me home, every afternoon Socks and I
got to walk around the property together. She didn't have much
energy, so we walked slowly. We meandered around the neighborhood. She sat by my side in the sun while Jay and I planted a
vegetable garden. In the evenings we all snuggled and watched
movies.

Socks had told me that she would give me another year and
train my next companion dog. I didn't want another companion dog! I could not imagine having such a deep relationship
with anyone else but my girl. I was resolved to never have another service dog again.

But at the start of the pandemic my father found himself
retired and strictly quarantined to protect himself. He lived
alone and needed a companion, so he decided to get himself
an Australian shepherd puppy. We had an Australian shepherd
when I was growing up, and he was an amazing friend. My dad
was older now and had probably forgotten what it took to raise
a herding dog with so much energy. Within a few weeks the
puppy, named Sky, had proven himself to be way too much for
my dad, who reached out to me and asked for help. "El, please
come get this puppy now!" he pleaded.

Not in the market for a puppy, Jay and I figured we would
take the Aussie home and help him get adopted. When we met
him for the first time, we were surprised at how affectionate he
was. Sky hurled himself at us and licked our faces so much we
could hardly breathe. His whole body was wagging, and it felt
much more like a reunion than an introduction. Without any

hesitation, the pup followed us to the car, jumped into my lap, and happily snoozed in my arms for the drive home. Within the sixty minutes it took us to pull into our driveway, Jay and I had both fallen hard in love with this little ball of gray, white, brown, and black fluff.

Socks greeted this little arrival like she had known him forever and had been anticipating this reunion. At that moment, I realized with stinging surprise that the little Aussie was the service dog Socks had planned to train all along.

Socks showed Sky when it was appropriate to play and when he needed to be more focused and calm. She acclimated him to our barnyard animals and to our guests, teaching him to be respectful and kind. She modeled for him how to follow me everywhere and sit next to me. Socks raised him from a young puppy full of energy to a professional dog who could be trusted to go with me anywhere.

By then it was summer and deliciously warm. Socks had executed every item on her bucket list except going to the beach. Cheyanne and I packed up the car with towels, blankets, bowls for food and water, and snacks for us all. I was tempted but decided not to take any of our other dogs. I wanted this day to be special for Socks and for her to have our undivided attention.

Barefoot, warm sand between our toes, carrying things in both arms, and moving slowly for Socks, it took a while to make the hundred-yard walk from where we could park to the shoreline. When we finally arrived, we picked a spot on the dry sand to spread the blanket, set up the food, water, and chairs, and settled down to relax in the sun and listen to the ocean's roar. The misty air from the surf seemed to revive Socks, and her energy reminded me of her adventurous and uncontainable spirit once more. She leaped over incoming waves, played "catch me if you can" with the seagulls, and had a smile on her face for hours. I thought for sure her increased activity would give her an appetite, but she didn't eat a bite, even of the Beyond Meat burger we picked up on the way that had always been her favorite.

On the drive home, now windswept, suntanned, and sleepy, I felt my mood take a sudden swing, from relaxed to frightened and really sad. I looked in the rearview mirror into the face of the dog who had brought me so much joy, security, support, and love. I gripped the wheel as my heart began to ache, knowing this would be her last trip by my side; the beach day was the final item on her bucket list, and the calendar year had now gone by. She had kept her promise to me, and I had kept mine to her.

A few days later Socks stopped eating completely. I still took her to the animal hospital, hoping there was a way to keep her with me for a few more months, even though I knew no amount of time would ever make my life the same without her. The veterinarian told me there was nothing they could do at this point. My only course of action now was to keep her comfortable and honor her wishes when she was ready to go.

On her last day physically with us, Socks was unable to stand or walk. I told her that her last hours should be whatever she wanted. She told me she would like to go with joy and happiness, not sorrow. She didn't want us to be in pain. She didn't want us to cry for her. She wanted us to celebrate her life. She wanted us to cherish our wonderful times together and the beautiful, slow goodbye we had been given. Her final wish was to have a farewell parade.

We carried her to our golf cart and sat her in the front seat, between Jay and me, with our kids in the back seat, and drove her around the property while the other dogs romped, played, and ran beside us. We drove past the horses and donkeys she had known for over a decade. We drove past the cows she had always greeted gently. We drove past the smaller animal barnyard and saw the chickens, pigs, turkeys, goats, and sheep who had all come to know her through the fence while she waited for me during tours. She got to see the blue sky and feel the fresh air on her face. By the time we drove back to the house, we were all smiling. The parade truly was a celebration of her magnificent life.

The vet arrived as we were carrying Socks back into the house to lay her on her dog bed. While the veterinarian prepared the syringes and medications, we all gathered around her and thanked her, one by one, for all the love and kindness she had given us, and we took turns speaking of our favorite memories with her. It took me back to something I had heard years before.

Before we purchased and built up our Santa Clarita location, I had started the Gentle Barn in the small half-acre that was my backyard in the San Fernando Valley. One day, I crossed paths with a neighbor and asked how she was.

"Phenomenal," she answered with a smile.

"Oh, wow! Why are you doing so great?" I asked.

I expected that she had bought a new car, had a special lunch with a friend, or maybe won the lottery. I'm sure my jaw dropped open when she answered that she had just said good-bye to her beloved dog.

Somehow, I managed to choke out the only question I could think of: "How can you be so happy about losing your loved one?"

She explained to me that her dog's transition was not a tragedy. They shared the most beautiful bond, and her dog had a great life and a peaceful, lovely passing. It was the picture-perfect life. She told me that having the honor of fulfilling her dog's last wishes and setting her free was the most beautiful thing she'd ever experienced.

I am sure I smiled halfheartedly but walked away thinking that she had to be insane to think that something as painful as death could ever be happy. Losing a loved one made me distraught and created suffering. I had no concept then of death being a time of beauty and release.

In Socks's final minutes, as we walked her home, I could finally understand what that neighbor had tried to explain years before. Nothing was left unsaid or undone between me and Socks — we knew how we felt about each other because we had spent so much time together. Socks had a long and wonderful life filled with adventure, affection, purpose, family, and happiness. She guarded and guided, played, fulfilled her bucket list, and then prepared me to be without her by mentoring young Sky. She passed away at home in her bed, with her family around her, after a parade. It was a picture-perfect life, and all I felt was gratitude, both for Socks's life and for another precious gift: the realization that if the life and the transition of a loved one is beautiful, then their death can be beautiful too.

I have come to see that loving our animals is like going on a vacation to the most luxurious, gorgeous, and exotic destination we can imagine, with the perfect people, in the perfect place, with the perfect amenities. When we return home from that vacation, we don't cry at the fact that our vacation is over, but rather we sit with smiles on our faces, sharing pictures and stories, holding on to all the beautiful memories we have created.

Most of us will experience the death of an animal companion. Instead of avoiding or fearing death, we could recognize that saying farewell to our animals is most likely a certainty and let go of worrying about it.

While our animals are with us, we can let them know we love them by spending as much quality time with them as possible. Then, when the time comes, we can try to make their passing peaceful and easy. When our loved ones can have a beautiful life and an easy passing, that is not a tragedy but a fairy tale.

CHAPTER NINE

PATSY, LIGHT, DAVID, AND VICTORY

We may not be able to see the mosaic yet,
but we need to have faith that we are all pieces
that come together to make a beautiful picture.

— LIGHT

While the pandemic was raging around the globe, Jay and I, along with the citizens of the world, mourned the loss of many people. There was nothing we could do to change the larger circumstances; however, during these long months of low human-to-human contact, we had the time and opportunity to save the tiniest of lives.

We found a baby mouse, the size of a thumb, lying in our backyard with a head injury. We held the baby for weeks while she repaired and gained strength, at first feeding her liquid food from a dropper and then cheering her recovery as she ate tiny pieces of food while perched on one of our fingers. When she was finally healed and active, we released her to the backyard where we'd found her. To this day I maintain a little shed in my backyard for her, with clean water, fresh food, and a warm bed of blankets for when she needs a haven to rest in.

At around this time, someone found a large egg on a golf course following a rainstorm and brought it to the Gentle Barn. We set the egg up in a borrowed incubator to see if there was life inside. After a few weeks, we gathered around in awe, staying up all night to watch as a perfect little Canada goose made her way out of the shell and greeted us as if we were her parents. She slept in the crook of our necks and followed us around everywhere, growing fast, flapping her wings, and getting stronger. As much as we all loved her, we knew she needed to follow her instincts and be free to swim, migrate, mate for life, and have her own babies. At several weeks old, with the help of a wildlife rescue organization, we found a family of Canada geese with goslings her age, and the mom and dad adopted her. Watching her grow in the egg, hatch, explore, and join a goose family of her own was a privilege and a gift from the pandemic.

Another person brought us a newly hatched orphan chick to raise. Cheyanne took charge as the parent figure for the little ball of saffron fuzz, and Meep was raised in our house, slept in our beds, cuddled in our laps, watched television when we did, and traveled in the car with us to movie theaters, restaurants, and other people's houses. We were a fully attentive chicken family for several months, until he acclimated to the barnyard and befriended the other animals, choosing to sleep outside with them. Having a house chicken is the best!

A pigeon who had been shot and could not fly came to live with us right before the pandemic began. He was a hilarious member of our large menagerie! Our heads became his landing pad, or he would follow us from room to room, cooing and trying to get our attention. Pushing items off the countertop became his entertainment, and a shiny appliance would become his obsession as he flirted with his own reflection with inappropriate gestures. If you needed a good laugh, Fern always provided the reason.

At one point in the middle of the three-year pandemic, I felt like my dreams were all coming true. We had barnyards full of cows, horses, sheep, donkeys, goats, pigs, llamas, turkeys, and chickens, as well as a peacock and an emu. Living inside with us were the dogs, a cockatoo, a pigeon, a baby chick, a little gosling, and a tiny field mouse. Everything I had imagined at age seven was now my authenticated reality over four decades later.

The restrictions of the pandemic also gave me a beautifully timed opportunity to authenticate my life in a whole new way. Though I had listened to animals whisper to me since I was a child, I still hadn't given myself the full credit of calling myself an animal communicator. I had listened to and connected with hundreds of animals by that point, but I didn't have enough confidence in my abilities to talk about my skill to help other people. A few years before, I had started a friendship with Joan Ranquet, an animal communicator, author, and founder of Communication with All Life University, where she teaches animal communication and energy healing to people around the world. Joan graciously invited me to take part in her two-year animal communication course. She thought taking the course would deepen my confidence.

Joan lives right around the corner from me, so I gratefully accepted her offer and soon found that learning animal communication, connecting to my intuition, believing in myself, and taking myself seriously was the best opportunity for self-discovery and growth I had ever experienced. Joan's school changed my life and validated my animal communication skills, and afterward Jay generously set me up with a website, and with his encouragement, I started doing animal communication professionally. With this work I am helping people and animals, loving every minute of it, and finally feeling unabashedly aligned with who I am and who I was always supposed to be!

The Gentle Barn programs had to be put on pause during lockdown, and our usual Sundays, filled with happy visitors, had to be temporarily shut down. Many of our volunteers and most of our staff were also quarantining at home or limiting their contact with others. We were operating with far fewer crew members but double the number of animals needing rescue. Jay and I had to work very hard, often twenty hours a day, to keep these animals alive.

No one had any idea how long the pandemic would last, and the fear of an economic downturn spread across the meat and dairy industries. The farmers did not want to get stuck with animals they could not turn to profit, so they sold off whole herds, sending them to be "processed," which quickly overwhelmed the slaughterhouses, also threatening to close down.

Because these cows were all kept pregnant, they were either slaughtered pregnant or gave birth at the slaughterhouse. The owner of a Los Angeles slaughterhouse would call us when a baby was born inside his facility because Jay had established a relationship with him. At first, the owner would offer to give us the baby only and keep the mother, but Jay, with kind and persistent negotiation skills, finally got him to agree that we would take the mom along with her baby. The owner held to this arrangement for many years.

He called us often during the pandemic.

The first animals that came to us from the slaughterhouse were two cows who had given birth in the slaughterhouse holding pen. We gave the moms the names Patsy and Light. Patsy's baby was a sickly little girl whom we called Victory, and Light's baby boy, equally unwell, was given the name David. We expected both Patsy and Light to be traumatized by their experience awaiting death in the crowded pens, and imagined they would be unapproachable and terrified. Often rescued animals are very hard to take care of because they won't let a human being close enough to dress their wounds or give them medication. Somehow, however, both Patsy and Light seemed to sense that they had been spared and were in a safe place. We were able to gain their trust quickly, and their sweet personalities gave us permission to treat them and care for their babies.

The babies were three or four days old by the time the slaughterhouse released them to us. Being without care or clean bedding, in crowded and chaotic circumstances, the cows were all in bad shape when Jay picked them up. They had pneumonia with extremely high fevers, and an infection had settled into Victory's joints, making it painfully hard for her to stand or walk.

The calves could nurse from their moms, but often their fevers were so high or they were so weak they couldn't stay upright long enough to finish. I fed them more with bottles to ensure the right amount of nutrition. From sunup to sundown, I stayed in the stall with Patsy, Light, Victory, and David. I cleaned their bedding, filled their water bowls, and replenished their hay. I gave them antibiotic injections, took their temperatures several times a day, did energy healing, and sang to them. I did all this alone, while Jay took care of the household and the other animals. Someone would usually bring me lunch. Joan visited me and did energy healing with me, and other energy healers we knew supported my efforts with remote energy healing for the babies. I was grateful for any help I could get.

Soon all this appeared to be having a positive effect, as both calves started to gain strength, could stand to nurse more often, and even began to play and explore. One morning, Victory was able to run in a full gallop, kicking up her heels and jumping in the air. She ran around and around Patsy and Light in circles, and we all watched mesmerized.

Some animals run and play because they are truly recovered. Other animals may have a short time of physical rallying right before they get worse. Sure enough, the next day, Victory's fever came back with a vengeance. The infection in her joints increased to its highest level and she slumped to the ground, barely able to stand or breathe. The vet came out every day to see her, trying new treatments until one day she said it was cruel to keep Victory in her state of illness. We had to let her go.

Walking Victory home was a crushing sorrow for me. Even though the vet reminded us that the survival rate for sickly calves is often less than 50 percent, that had not stopped my heart from encompassing this tender little girl, taking her in as if she were my own. I had clung to every glimpse of progress. I had convinced myself that we had rounded the corner and she was in the clear. It was what *should* happen. Babies are supposed to live, thrive, and have wonderful lives. Out of the jaws of the darkest place on earth, Victory had been brought to the Gentle Barn, and here she was supposed to have a living apology for what they all had been through at the slaughterhouse. When we brought Patsy and Light home, we promised them they would have their babies for the rest of their lives. Victory never got her living apology, and Patsy never got her lifelong motherhood.

After Patsy nuzzled her baby goodbye, Jay carried Victory's lifeless body outside and placed her under a tree, so I could say goodbye to her as well. This love I had nurtured and delighted in was now only a form without breath or a heartbeat. I lay on the ground near her sweet face and sobbed.

"You've got it all wrong!" I heard someone whisper in my ear.

Stunned, I stopped crying and sat up to see who was speaking. No one was nearby.

I lay back down, barely daring to breathe as I hoped to hear more.

The voice continued, "This is not a tragedy. This is a gift. Victory came to spend three beautiful weeks with you. She came from the slaughterhouse to feel the love at the Gentle Barn. She didn't die at the slaughterhouse but got to have her mom and you beside her when she left. It was a three-week gift for her and for you. Be grateful."

I didn't know if I was receiving this message from my higher self, from Buddha or Dudley, or if Victory's own sweet spirit was consoling my heart. But it did console me, and from this baby cow I learned another elevated way to perceive death even when life is only a month long. Sometimes loved ones come to us for a very short time, to visit. Because we expect children and animals to have a certain life span, we look at it as a tragedy when their lives are shortened.

Victory came for a short time, by our earthly standards, but she brought a gift of immense proportion. I thanked her, kissing her soft ear, and then stood up and took a deep breath. I knew that to move forward, I would have to take my focus off her short life span and turn it to gratitude for having known her, for having loved her and shown her the joy of the Gentle Barn.

Every day after that, I watched as little David continued to grow stronger, nursing from both his mom, Light, and also from Patsy, and every night I watched as the two moms groomed him and slept by his side.

At our sanctuary, male animals need to be neutered. We don't breed animals here because if we have room for more, we want to rescue them, not bring more into the world. Usually, a baby male cow is neutered early on, but David had such a rocky beginning to life, I wanted to wait several months to make sure he was big and strong enough to make the surgery relatively inconsequential for him.

When the time was right, our veterinarian came out to do the procedure. He is a world-renowned surgeon who specializes in safely using anesthesia in surgeries for compromised animals. Before the procedure, I spoke intuitively to Light and explained what we were doing and why. Even for a thirty-minute neuter, I didn't want to put her through the trauma of being separated from her baby, so we put David in the adjoining pen so Patsy and Light could be right there to watch.

The sedation went fine, and David lay down peacefully, his breathing normal. The doctor started the neutering. Everything was going well. After about twenty-five minutes, the doctor looked up at me and said, "I'm putting the final stitches in, and in a few minutes, we're going to wake David up."

Up to that point, I had been feeding Patsy and Light cookies and reassuring them. I thought this was a good opportunity to check in with David. I sat at the back of the barn, out of everybody's way, closed my eyes, and connected with him. I said, "David, how are you doing?"

He answered, "I am fine. It is so beautiful here." He felt expanded and peaceful.

"That's great, David. Take a few more minutes to enjoy, but then it'll be time to come back to your body."

"I don't want to."

It seemed like something a child outside at play would say to a parent. I gently persuaded him. "I don't blame you at all. But your moms need you, we need you, and the world needs to learn from your story to be kinder to animals. In a few minutes, I'm going to want you to start coming back to your body."

David stomped his feet and said firmly and decisively, "*No! I am not coming back!*"

Moments later our vet called loudly from across the barn, "He's arresting. I am starting CPR."

Panic welled up inside of me, and I started arguing with David in my mind. "Cut it out. Knock it off. This isn't funny. I need you back in your body right now."

"No," David said. "I'm not coming back!"

Our doctor did CPR for twenty minutes, until he was exhausted and covered in sweat. He finally called it quits, declaring David deceased.

Stunned, I instantaneously began blaming myself for David's death. I'm the one who promised Patsy and Light they would have their babies as long as they lived at the Gentle Barn. Victory's passing was beyond my control, but David's neuter was an elective surgery, one that I chose for him.

I knew that it's not possible to maintain a sanctuary for animals without neutering the males, but how would I ever have the courage to neuter the next one? I felt hopeless, over-whelmed by this unexpected loss, and wanted to quit the Gentle Barn. I went home in a stunned stupor, got into bed, and told Jay that I wasn't coming out. I was exhausted by life, and by death.

I had experienced compassion fatigue before and now rec-ognized the symptoms. I knew that it gave me a hopeless feel-ing of wanting to give up all together. My rational mind could recognize what was happening, but that didn't lessen the emo-tional pain of losing David. I gave myself twenty-four hours to fall apart, to shut out the world and grieve, and then promised myself that after indulging in my feelings, I would reach out for help and pick myself back up.

The next day, I told Joan about losing David. She did a ses-sion of Emotional Freedom Technique, or tapping, with me. Using a blend of acupressure points on the top of my head, on my face, and on my breastbone area, she spoke statements that helped me release the trauma of the debilitating loss. When she finished, I felt lighter. I was so impressed with the experience and so inspired by the idea that tapping could be used equally well on animals that I later learned the technique myself so I could offer it, along with animal communication, to my clients to help their animals recover from their trauma.

Even though I felt lighter, I still needed to understand why David had to pass away. It just seemed so cruel. It shook my confidence as a rescuer, healer, and leader. I had hired the very best veterinarian, with the very best anesthesia, and did it in the most thoughtful way, and still he passed away. Why?!

Many times before I had gone for hope and healing to Lara Arguigo, a friend who is an energy healer. I was still having a hard time with David's death, so I asked for her help. She took me through a beautiful guided meditation, where I found wis-dom and fantastic answers to all my questions.

During the meditation, one thought in particular gave me great clarity. Life on planet Earth is like a mosaic. When we look at one individual piece of a mosaic, it doesn't look like much more than a piece of broken tile or a random shape that doesn't hold any particular meaning on its own. When we step back, however, and look at the whole mosaic, made up of various colors and placement of tiles, we can see that they all come together to make a beautiful picture. When we look at any small segment of our lives, like one event or one person or animal, we may not understand the larger purpose. When we step back and look at everyone's lives intersecting, interacting, and affecting each other, a beautiful mural of larger meaning comes into view.

We will never understand all the secrets of this universe while we are in our physical form. I believe that those on the other side can see the bigger picture, but we must go through our lives one piece at a time, the joy-filled moments as well as those that cause us unbearable sorrow. Then one day we too will cross over and be able to see how everything fits together to make sense.

My healing through Lara and with Joan reminded me that there are three parts to rescue work: the animals' own will and desire to live, our capabilities and efforts to save them, and what the Universe wishes. If an animal does not want to be here, no amount of effort will save them. That is why we do so much to help them want to live. We also provide the best food, water, shelter, and veterinary care available, as well as all our love. That's the second part. Sometimes, though, even if the first and second pieces are in place, the animal still might not make it because of the third component. We will never understand why or for how long someone else is supposed to be here. That is something only our loved one and the Universe understand.

I was raised to study and work as hard as I could, watching my dad sacrifice time with his family, relaxation, and self-care to be the best at what he did. My father was indeed at the top of his field, becoming the chief of cardiac surgery at UCLA and saving thousands of lives over the course of his career. At the Gentle Barn I had the same work ethic, working as hard as I could and sacrificing everything to help as many animals and people as possible.

Without an understanding and a practice of self-care, my work ethic (or my overwork ethic) became a problem for me. I used to think that compassion fatigue was just extreme sadness, stress, or overwhelm, and I didn't realize how profound its effects could be. When I experienced it myself for the first time, I was so affected and surprised by it that it took months to overcome. Still, it wasn't until I was fifty-one years old that I recognized the need for true self-care.

The foothills in Southern California are prone to wildfires, especially in times of drought. The dry grasses and bushes of the hillsides are brittle tinder for fast-spreading fires. In 2019 a nearby fire spread quickly until, within just forty minutes, it was dangerously close to us. We were faced with a wall of fire that could leap across the street at any moment and trap us on our own property. Calling on the kindness of volunteers and staff, even strangers, we somehow managed to evacuate the animals while Jay and some of the other staff held the fire at bay with hoses, shovels, and fire extinguishers. Once the animals were safe and the fire department had put out the flames, we spent six days awake and on alert, watching to make sure there were no sparks left to reignite.

With the exhaustion and strain on my body, I came down with an illness that I now think was Covid, even before it was recognized as being present in the United States. I was severely ill for four grueling days, unable to do anything but groan in bed. Once I had recovered from the throbbing headache and high fever, I became extremely anemic and started passing out. I went back to work, expecting to bounce back soon. But over the next several days I grew so weak that I could not even stand up to get dressed, much less work.

Ignoring the severity of my physical condition, I decided to work sitting down. It wasn't until I was completely yellow, out of breath, and passing out constantly that Jay insisted I go to the hospital. Even then, I fought the idea, wanting to stay home to continue working.

At the emergency room, the front desk person took one look at me and admitted me right away, recognizing that I could lose my life without intervention. I spent the next week getting three blood transfusions and stern lectures from the doctor and everyone in my family about taking better care of myself.

This near-death experience made me step back to look at the larger mosaic of my own being. By focusing on the high-priority day-to-day needs of others, I had allowed myself to go into deep denial about my need for self-care. It's not that I was on the bottom of my list of those I loved and cared for — I wasn't on my list at all!

Since then, I have come to understand compassion fatigue as way more than just stress. I now recognize its symptoms and know how to pull myself out of it, faster and faster each time. I have come to accept that compassion fatigue is and will always be part of my work. Those of us who are empaths, warriors, caregivers, lightworkers, and healers, those of us who self-sacrifice, feel the pain of others, and give all that we have away, are going to see the suffering and cruelty of this world, and eventually we will feel hopeless and defeated. It is futile to resist or avoid it, but we all must know how to survive it.

I have watched as other gifted rescuers and caregivers, suffering the effects of compassion fatigue, eventually quit and walk away from their work of good. This isn't the solution; the environment, the animals, and all the world's innocents need us now more than ever. If we know how to get through compassion fatigue, we can keep going to help even more.

Like most people, I had no option to walk away. My children, animals, employees, volunteers, and followers were counting on my strength. So I came up with a five-part plan to minimize the effects of compassion fatigue and prevent my work from zapping the life from me.

First, I decided to share my message more gently, so that I would live in harmony all the time. I would not indulge my feelings of upset at the state of the world because that only hurt me and didn't have a positive effect on anyone else. I worked on staying gentle and calm, taking responsibility for my reactions.

Second, after sharing my message gently, I had to lose attachment to the outcome. What people did with their experience at the Gentle Barn or the knowledge they gained there was their concern, not mine. Their journey was none of my business. I could control only *my* choices.

Third, I had to surround myself with people, experiences, and news that uplifted, inspired, and encouraged me. I pledged to stop watching and listening to the news. I began to follow only uplifting pages on social media. I became extremely picky about what shows and movies I watched, and I created an inner circle of friends who would always leave me feeling encouraged.

Fourth, I committed to celebrating the victories. In every cause, the finish line seems so far away, and the problem so huge. Often we are so overwhelmed by the problem that we don't acknowledge that we are making strides every day. In my cause of peace, love, and joy for animals, there are new vegan products, restaurants, spokespeople, and other accomplishments every day. I gave myself permission to celebrate those victories, no matter how small.

Fifth and finally, I came up with a meditation to help create a peaceful planet. I based it on my vision for the Gentle Barn, which I had long manifested each night before I went to bed. After years of imagining what the Gentle Barn would be like, I could practically taste, smell, and touch it in my mind. And then it came to be! If that worked to create the Gentle Barn, then I could do the same thing to create a peaceful planet. Each morning I set my alarm for five minutes, sat comfortably, closed my eyes, and visualized clean oceans, thriving marine life, tall ancient trees, safe animals, gardens and orchards that nourish humanity, horses running free, and people cradling chickens, cuddling turkeys, hugging cows, and holding hands peacefully with each other. Every conversation, experience, or ounce of work I did afterward was born out of that intention, that dream. I still do this every morning, and I will continue visualizing that peaceful, gentle world until we have it.

Along with my five-part plan, I set up a toolbox to help me recover from compassion fatigue. Inside I put the names of everyone who can help me in a crisis: energy healers, tarot card readers, mediums, therapists, and friends. Then I added a list of simple, easy, affordable things that bring me joy, like taking a bubble bath, walking in nature, spending time with my family, meditating, and of course being in my barnyard. Being aware of those things and writing them down reminded me to do them regularly, and to do them all to help me heal when I was in crisis. I then added a list of the things I had accomplished so far, to remind me of the importance of continuing, even when I felt broken. This little toolbox is stashed away somewhere safe, and when compassion fatigue hits next, I'll reach inside and take out the tools to help me recover, heal, and keep going.

So often, self-care is associated with working to be perfect. It's about losing weight or getting a manicure; it's what we do to feel like we look good enough or have accomplished enough compared to other people. That type of self-care landed me in the hospital. My new self-care toolkit — the five-part plan and the toolbox — began with the premise that self-care has to start with self-love. Slowly and steadily, for the first time in my life, I committed to love and nurture myself. Instead of picking myself apart in the mirror, I started appreciating my body for what it had been for me. My breasts had nursed, nourished, and fed two children, establishing their strong immune systems. My legs allowed me to do my work and walk among my animals. My arms allowed me to embrace the broken, lost, and sick rescues we bring in and give them safety. My wrinkles were trophies, memories of the many times I had smiled, laughed, frowned, and cried because I had loved so much and so many. My gray hairs were ribbons of honor for all that I have grown through, experienced, evolved, and learned.

I have never heard an animal complain about their bodies. They never say that they are too fat, too thin, too old, too young, too short, or too tall, like we tend to do. They accept themselves the way they are, are grateful for what their bodies can do and thankful to be alive. They eat when they are hungry, drink when thirsty, sleep when tired, and spend most of their day doing what makes them happy. I realized that the way we talk to ourselves is vicious, and I would never speak to anyone else the way I spoke to myself. It was time to be kinder to myself. It was time to be more like my animals.

I pledged to feed my body fresh organic fruits, vegetables, nuts, and grain, and exercise my body so I could be stronger and have more energy. I added myself to the list of those I love and care for, treating myself like I would any of my kids or animals.

As empaths, lightworkers, caregivers, healers, nurses, firefighters, doctors, veterinarians, police officers, rescuers, animal lovers, moms, and dads, we have lives depending on us every day. We need to give more to ourselves so we can give more to others. We need to care for ourselves first, and then extend all the care, nurturing, and acceptance outward. Love is an inside job…and we deserve it.

CHAPTER TEN

JOHN LEWIS THUNDERHEART

This world is magic — always remember the gratitude.

— JOHN LEWIS THUNDERHEART

During the hot midsummer months of 2020, I found myself sitting on the floor of my living room in a homemade oxygen tent. It wasn't Covid; it was a calf.

Jay and I, along with our kids, have at various times shared our home living spaces with a chicken or two, a pigeon, dogs, a cockatoo, a dove, and miscellaneous human friends, family, volunteers, and staff. But this was the first time a cow had crossed the threshold and become long-stay company.

In late July we had received another call from the slaughterhouse owner. A baby who had been born in the holding area needed to be picked up within hours if we wanted to save him. I was still emotionally bruised from losing Victory and David only months before, but there was no way we wouldn't bring this new baby home.

While I stayed behind to prepare another little nursery in our Sun Chlorella Healing Center, Jay got ready to rescue the baby and also the mom. As he was getting into his truck, I told him, "An image of a golden calf came to my mind right after the phone call."

We had not been given any descriptions of the mom or the baby, just that it was urgent that we get there. I had sensed the arrivals of other animals before we rescued them, but I had never been given a direct and clear visual image like this. I also had a strong intuitive feeling that this new arrival would be important to our lives.

As was our usual agreement with the slaughterhouse owner, Jay expected to take the mother along with the baby, but this time they refused to release the mother. The owner explained to Jay that the mother was ill and close to dying, and it was legally impossible for him to release her. Jay pleaded anyway, offering to sign a waiver and pay whatever money she would have brought in, but the owner stood firm: We could only take the baby.

After he made the baby comfortable in the trailer, Jay pulled over to the side of the road to call and tell me that he was indeed golden and to deliver the sad news that the mother would not survive. In my heart, I sent this critically ill mama a message of gratitude and told her that we would do everything we could to save her son.

Upon his arrival I was instantly captivated by this golden calf with long, elegant legs, a fluffy tail, a sweet brown nose, two white socks on his back legs, and huge soft eyes laced with golden lashes. He was gorgeous!

After my experience with David and Victory, I knew that this baby too had pneumonia. He was dehydrated and had a severely high fever and raspy breathing. To protect my heart, I decided I would hold my expectations in check and not yearn for a regular, twenty-year life span for this calf, as I did with David. If this baby was meant to be with us for only one day, one week, one month, I was going to be grateful for the time we had. I pledged to take each day as it came. I was going to surrender to the Universe and whatever his journey was supposed to be, would be, with no hopes of my own. I was here to serve him.

Our wonderful veterinarians got started right away with antibiotics, anti-inflammatory medications, and a long set of instructions for us to follow daily. By the first week of August the outside temperature soared to 106 degrees, and the calf's fever spiked along with it. The antibiotics were no longer effective, and it seemed we were out of options for saving him.

"Let's move him into our house," Jay and I both said, out loud, in unison. I'm sure Jay wasn't at all surprised that *I* would come up with that idea, but it blew me away that he was thinking it too. I've always been the dreamer, and Jay the pragmatist. In this case, however, Jay and I were on the same page.

We moved all the furniture out of the living room, except for the couch, set up a little fenced area to keep him contained, and covered the floor with puppy pads that our generous followers had sent in for the cause. Then we got the baby calf, put him in the back seat of our car, and drove him from our Healing Center to our house. Our dog Sky and I sat with him in the back seat to keep him company while Jay drove.

Mother cows and their babies are together all the time. As an orphan, he needed round-the-clock companionship. So I was moving downstairs to become his mom. Sky, who never left my side, came too, and together we joined forces to save the life of the cow in our living room.

Once he was settled in the living room, the golden calf had a busy care routine. I took his temperature and gave him his medication three times a day, reported daily to the veterinarian, and used the nebulizer twice a day to help him breathe. Jay built a homemade oxygen tent from plastic sheeting and PVC, and the calf and I would sit under it each day to heal his lungs and give his body a fighting chance to rid itself of the infection. Every two hours, all through the day and night, I gave him a bottle — a mixture of fresh, raw, unpasteurized milk, which he should have been getting from his mom, and Sun Chlorella Algae Super Food to boost his immune system. Like any new mom with a newborn baby, I slept when he slept. I sang to him and loved him just like I would any baby.

Every time he finished a bottle, I would clean up the puppy pads and put fresh ones down. Then the little calf would lie down while I spooned his back and Sky snuggled up against us both…and we would all sleep. In exactly two hours I would open my eyes to find two brown eyes staring into mine, inches from my face, letting me know he was hungry. I would get up, warm up another bottle, and so it went repeatedly all night and all day. Jay would bring me food, and Cheyanne would keep us company after school. Being a momma cow was very engaging, and I loved every minute.

I did energy work on the calf and communicated with him in the same way I had with Ferdinand, in his early health struggles. I spent hours every day painting the picture of his future life. I sent him mental images: him galloping around, jumping into the air with his strong legs, being encircled by other cows who would protect him and surrounded by people who would love him.

Our social media followers really like the opportunity to submit names for newly rescued animals. As a simple way to raise funds for the animal's care, one small donation at a time, we hold a naming auction. People around the world send in their favorite name, which a staff member writes on paper, folds up, and places in a bucket or hat. Then, on a social media live stream, Jay holds up the container and I close my eyes, reach in, and randomly pick a piece of folded paper. I always trust that the perfect name will be chosen for our new rescue, and, as always, this was true for our little golden calf.

Earlier in the month, Senator John Lewis of Georgia, a lifelong civil rights leader, had passed away. An inspired leader, he had faced a lot of adversity in his younger years and went on to alter the world's views of race relations through his peaceful activism. It seemed magical that "John Lewis" was the name selected from the bucket. And because so many people had been following our posted videos on the little calf's progress, we decided to also pick a middle name, which became "Thunderheart." We called him Lewis for short.

There was yet more naming to do. It only seemed right that the mother cow who had brought us the gift of John Lewis Thunderheart should also be given a name, posthumously. Knowing we would be talking about her and carrying her with us for the rest of Lewis's life, we asked our followers to submit names for her. Miraculously, out of hundreds of tiny bits of folded paper, we picked out the name Love.

Soon after, when John Lewis Thunderheart was shaved for an ultrasound, Jay trimmed the square bald patch into a shapely heart as a reminder that Love was always with him. We maintain the shaved heart on Lewis's side to this day.

While I was completely focused and happily raising a calf in my house, I never lost sight of the fact that people worldwide were losing their jobs, businesses were closing down, many had to move in with other family members, all modes of travel were restricted, the health care system was strained, thousands every week became sick with Covid, and many died alone. Fear and stress had no outlets, and people were suffering mentally and emotionally.

Our followers sought comfort from our videos and live feeds about John Lewis. He seemed to be a beacon of hope. Watching his will to live and seeing him get stronger and grow each day was giving people something positive to focus on in the worst days of the pandemic. Hundreds of thousands of viewers from around the world tuned in every day for a John Lewis update. We made daily videos of our simple and comforting routines with him: sharing songs, story time, bottle time, and bedtime tuck-in.

By September, though he still had raspy breathing and a strong cough, Lewis started needing bottles less often. He weaned himself, from a bottle every two hours to four times a day and then down to three. Eventually we were all able to sleep through the night.

The vet kept making me cautiously aware that this was not going to be a quick fix, and it would take John Lewis a long time to fully recover. We were under strict instructions not to take him outside during the heat of the day, as it would compromise his lungs. Once the sun went down, however, we were cleared to play in the backyard. I would put his tiny purple halter on him and lead him out the back door, down the back steps, and onto the lawn. Once I released him from his lead rope, Lewis and Sky would explore together like two puppies. They would chase each other, galloping back and forth, and wrestle gently with each other.

Cows play by bonking heads, and Lewis would bonk Sky with his head. Dogs play by gently nipping and interacting with their mouths, and Sky would gently nip and lick Lewis. Even though they spoke different languages, Lewis and Sky found a way to understand each other and forged a deep friendship.

After four months of countless sleepless nights, vet visits, ultrasounds, injections, thermometers, disposable puppy pads, and bottles, Lewis was finally declared healthy. We celebrated at first, and then we realized that being healthy meant it was time to neuter him.

I was still traumatized over what had happened to David, which had shown me that this elective procedure could kill a calf. Frankly, I was terrified. But if we kept my baby unneutered, Lewis would not be able to interact with the public, he would have to be kept away from female cows, and once grown, he might be unsafe for even me to handle. For him to have a family and a loved life, Lewis had to be neutered. I had to face my fears and cling to faith. It was so hard.

Unlike horses, goats, or sheep, who flee from danger, cows put their heads down and face their fears. They do not go into denial or avoidance, but rather they stare danger in the eyes. I had not exactly practiced this kind of courage before. I was much more the fight-or-flight kind of person. Now, having no other choice, I summoned my inner cow and booked the procedure.

Our veterinarian took excellent care not only of John Lewis but of me too. She kept reassuring me and talking me through the procedure. She kept telling me, "Just keep breathing, he's going to be fine, and you're going to be fine too."

As she was wrapping up the procedure, I closed my eyes and imagined a conversation with John Lewis's mother, Love. In my mind I asked her for permission to keep, raise, and love her baby in her honor. I promised to share his story with people around the world to open their hearts to cows everywhere. A calm came over me, I felt peaceful for the first time since I booked the procedure, and I had the feeling that Love was telling me "Yes."

A few minutes later, John Lewis woke from the anesthesia. He stood up, and I knew that he was mine.

Once Lewis had recovered from being neutered, we were given the green light to bring him outside during the day. We spent hours in the backyard, playing, racing, and exploring. At age six months, he started taking walks around our property with me to meet the cows who would eventually become his family.

Lewis would walk beside me on his purple lead rope, and Sky would run ahead and then circle back to get us, herding us the whole way. John Lewis would nibble on grass and lick tree trunks. One day Lewis discovered a big pile of fallen autumn leaves and lay right down in the middle of them. Sky and I joined him, and the three of us took a nap in the leaves for an hour.

Being with any baby reminds us to be in the present moment. It is almost impossible to rush a baby, especially a baby cow. When we took those walks together, I did not have an end goal, or a time frame, but allowed the moment to take us wherever it would, giving Lewis as much time as he needed to sniff, taste, and look at every little thing his heart desired. Looking through Lewis's eyes, I got to rediscover our property, with its tiny yellow flowers, random patches of grass, and beautiful little bushes I hadn't noticed before. In our stillness, I heard the chorus of birds filling the morning like a symphony and watched the pepper trees sway in the early morning breeze. Lewis taught me how to slow down and smell the roses, although in our case, it was more like "crunch the orange leaves."

As we passed the horse barn on our walks, Lewis went nose-to-nose with each horse and donkey. He was wide-eyed as he extended his neck out to them in humble greeting. The horses were curious about him too, and gentle in return, knowing he was a baby. More importantly, they knew he was my baby, and their respect for me bolstered their kindness for him. When we arrived at the cow pasture, all the cows would come to the fence, anxious to welcome him. Seeing the other cows towering over him reminded me that he was still very much a baby and had much more growing to do.

I brought Lewis to the cow pasture every day, for longer and longer stretches of time. For the first several weeks we visited the cows through the rails of the pasture fence. When Lewis and the other cows seemed comfortable with each other, we went into the pasture to visit with them. At first Lewis was hesitant and would stand behind me, peering out to watch. Eventually, he grew more comfortable and would approach the others if I were nearby.

Soon a new morning routine was falling in line. I called it "Cow Kindergarten." After his morning bottle, I would walk with Lewis down to the cow pasture, with Sky leading the way. I would stay in the pasture with him for a little while and then leave him in the nurturing and loving hands of my wonderful volunteers, who kept an eye on him while I went to work. Lewis was always happy to go and by this time was fully accepted by the other cows. In the afternoon, Sky and I would pick Lewis up and bring him back to the house for the rest of the evening and bedtime.

All babies learn from their mothers. As calves grow, they watch their mothers eat grass or hay and start nibbling on it themselves. Lewis had a human mom, who did not eat hay. He was very interested in eating my food but would not eat food fit for a cow. So for hours each evening, after Cow Kindergarten, Sky, Lewis, and I would sit outside in a big, soft pile of hay in our backyard, and I would graze on it like a cow. It was prickly at first, but once I chewed on it for a minute, it turned soft and palatable. It wasn't so bad. Lewis would watch me, until eventually he'd become curious enough to start nibbling on it too. I even had Sky trying it. After about two weeks, Lewis was eating hay in big mouthfuls. And then he began to eat his hay lunch beside the big cows. And one big cow in particular.

After Karma and then Crystal passed away, a cow named Holy Cow immediately stepped up as the herd's new matriarch, a position she still holds today. She was born into the dairy industry, taken away from her mom at birth, and put into a veal crate where she could not move. Not being able to exercise makes muscles soft, which apparently makes the veal more desirable. At eight weeks old, Holy Cow was scheduled to be slaughtered. But by the time she arrived at the auction house, she was so terribly sick that she couldn't even stand up. We brought her and another veal calf named Madonna home, and little by little, they both healed and grew into big, beautiful black and white cows.

Most animals who are not raised by mothers have difficulty being mothers when they grow up. Holy Cow, however, empathized with all the orphans we brought home and wanted to help them. From the time she was two years old, whenever we saved an orphan calf, we would give them to Holy Cow, and she would nurture them, groom them with her giant raspy tongue, and help us raise them.

When Sky and I first brought John Lewis down to the cow pasture, Holy Cow took one look at our little guy and called dibs. But when she tried to lick him, Lewis ran away from her. He didn't understand that kind of bonding because everything he'd learned, he'd learned from me.

Just as I had to eat hay to get John Lewis to eat it, I wondered if I would have to lick him so he would accept Holy Cow's gestures of friendship. I would have done anything for him, but as an intermediate step, I got a dog brush to see if I could brush him in the same pattern that Holy Cow would make with her tongue. Maybe I could get him used to that love language and convince him to let Holy Cow lick him? Each morning and evening after his bottle, I would brush Lewis in a rhythmic pattern, explaining to him as I went that this is what it would feel like to let Holy Cow lick him. I encouraged him to trust her and explained that she had a lot of love to give him.

Meanwhile Holy Cow didn't give up trying to show her affection. She would wait till he fell asleep and then tiptoe toward him with her neck outstretched and her tongue out, at the ready. Just as she was about to lick, Lewis would wake up from his nap and bolt out of the way. She tried to groom him every single day.

Finally, weeks later, John Lewis gave her a chance, standing still and allowing Holy Cow to get in her first licks. She was overjoyed and continued to pursue him in this way, until one day I found him soaking wet from head to tail and Holy Cow standing nearby with a very satisfied look in her eyes.

One sunny morning, when John Lewis Thunderheart was nine months old, I brought him to Cow Kindergarten after breakfast, dropped him off with the other cows, gave him a kiss and a hug goodbye, and wished him a wonderful day. When I returned at the end of the day and tried to walk him out of the cow pasture gate to return to our house, as I always did, he wouldn't budge. I applied more pressure to the lead rope, walked him in a circle, and tried luring him with grain and cookies. He still would not budge. After forty-five minutes of trying to make a 650-pound cow move when he didn't want to, I finally realized what he was trying to tell me: "I am a big cow now and want to sleep with my friends in the cow pasture."

When I unbuckled his halter, he bucked in the air and happily galloped back to the other cows. He looked back at me like a boy at a slumber party, saying, "Mom, I'm a big boy now." I was happy for him and smiling with pride, while at the same time mourning the fact that he wouldn't sleep in the house anymore.

In the same way Dudley did, John Lewis had become a treasured source of hope, determination, and joy to people around the world. I knew from the moment I first touched my little golden calf that he was here to heal. He healed my bruised heart from losing Victory and David, and he made a contri- bution to the larger community of human beings who were suffering through the pandemic. I knew the name John Lewis had been chosen because my little golden calf had a mission larger than staying in the safety of my arms. Still, like a mom who had just dropped her child off at college, tears splashed to the dusty path beneath my feet as I walked back up the hill to the house alone.

I kept John Lewis's beds and teddy bears in the house for another month, hoping he would change his mind and come back home. When he didn't, I brought his things down to the cow pasture for him. I continued to bring him his morning bottle. He was always very excited to see me, often waiting by the fence for me. When he saw me coming, his eyes got wide, his ears wiggled, and he danced back and forth with anticipation.

Lewis and I continued to cuddle after his bottle. He had weaned himself down to one bottle a day, and I had added more warm water and less milk until, by the time he was a year old, Lewis was enjoying warm water and Sun Chlorella to boost his immune system, without any milk at all. I would scratch all the favorite spots on his neck and shoulders and massage him. When we were done, he would slowly walk back to the hay bin or join the other cows. I still had a magical connection with my baby boy, but sadly I no longer had a cow in my living room.

CHAPTER ELEVEN

COW HUG THERAPY

There is a still, quiet, centered spot inside each of us
that we can all return to for healing when we just *be*.

— MADONNA

Human-to-human physical contact can often be awkward, but for someone who feels emotionally or physically vulnerable, even eye contact with other people can be overwhelming. As a little girl, eye contact alone would often make me feel judged or isolated. It was only with my animals that I could relax and know that I didn't have to be anything other than who I was, with whatever I was feeling.

Buddha, my first cow, was the source of my understanding of the healing power of Cow Hug Therapy: an opportunity to feel unconditional support, warmth, and safe nonjudgment at the side of a gentle healer. Because of a cow's large size, even adult humans can feel they are in a protector's care. Starting with Buddha, we established Cow Hug Therapy as a foundational offering at the Gentle Barn. Whether they were coming with a school field trip, as part of a private tour, or with a foster agency, homeless shelter, domestic violence shelter, or rehab center, our guests have always hugged our cows.

During the first years of the pandemic, when the Gentle Barn had to be closed to visitors, we received many emails and comments on social media from people saying they needed the love of our animals to help them through their hardship, both mentally and physically. One day an email arrived from a foster care caseworker, writing on behalf of a seventeen-year-old girl I'll call Mandy, who was in crisis. I thought of how incredibly hard the pandemic had been for our own teenage daughter and could not fathom how hard it must be for a child in foster care, without a secure family to call her own.

The caseworker wrote that being around animals was the only thing that lit Mandy up and made her feel that life was worth living. The caseworker acknowledged in her email that she knew we were closed due to the pandemic and not running our programs, but because Mandy was in such despair, she wondered if we might make an exception. I knew I would not say no, despite the Covid risks. When I weighed the risk of a young girl feeling hopeless and alone with the risk of me getting this virus while outside in the barnyard, I knew the answer. I would wear a mask and social distance, but this girl would get the comfort she needed with our animals.

When they arrived, I tried to look into the face of this beautiful young lady and make conversation. I told her it was nice to meet her and asked if she had ever been here before. She stared at the ground, wouldn't look at me, and wouldn't answer me. She was completely shut down. Not wanting her to feel awkward, I moved us on to meet the cows.

As we opened the gate to the pasture, Mandy's eyes were still cast on the ground, and she walked in the shadow of her caseworker. John Lewis, acting as if being reunited with a long-lost friend, came bounding over, full of life and fun, with a bright, mischievous expression on his face. I could hear Mandy start to giggle as he licked her arm, like a popsicle, and leaned his body against hers.

John Lewis took over from there, and Mandy responded immediately, stroking his neck, bowing her face toward his soft coat. In a matter of minutes, this despondent shell of a girl looked up at me for the first time and began asking questions: What's his name? What's his story? How old is he? Coincidentally, she and John Lewis shared the same birthday, July 23, and that made her smile from ear to ear.

After she had hugged Lewis close, I brought her over to

meet our older cows, who were lying down in anticipation of her arrival. I showed Mandy how to kneel down beside their shoulders, lean her weight onto their sides, put her face on their backs, close her eyes, breathe in and out a few times, and connect without words, without expectations, without thinking, just heart to heart, soul to soul, in silence. An hour later, my heart was full, seeing how Mandy had relaxed and connected in a way that melted the deep frown from between her eyes.

The Cow Hug Therapy was so successful that we set up a plan for Mandy to come back once a month. Sometimes we returned to the cows for cuddles, other times we groomed and walked horses, or we went to the upper barnyard and sat on the floor to give tummy rubs to pigs, hold chickens, or pat goats and sheep.

Mandy's arrivals were always a little bit awkward, human to human. She clearly didn't feel right in her own skin, which made it a bit hard to find our starting place. But the minute we got into the pastures or into the barnyards, a light shined in her eyes and she was full of questions and conversation. Little by little, with each visit, she would tell me more about her life, about what she was going through, what it was like in the foster homes, and what it was like in her home of origin. She even told me about her boyfriend.

The thread through all our conversations was always animals. She shared with me how she was ridiculed and misunderstood for her love of animals. She excitedly described the dog she wanted to get one day. She reminisced about animals she had known in former group homes, who always made her feel safe.

Over time I really got to know Mandy. I related to her completely, understanding what it is like to be a girl who only among animals felt she was worthy and really mattered. I was glad that I didn't have to sit on the Covid sidelines anymore.

I was finally helping somebody in the pandemic, and it felt wonderful.

John Lewis was the third cow in my life to wrap his neck around me and hold me for hours. Other than Buddha, Dudley, and John Lewis, there has never been another cow in the history of the Gentle Barn who did that for me. There were many orphan cows, baby cows, rescued cows that I would embrace and cuddle and spend time with, and I have had deep relationships with all the cows we have rescued. Some of them were scared and some took much longer to trust me, but I've come to know hundreds of cows. And there have been only three who wrapped their necks around me and held me in that way.

Not only does John Lewis cuddle me, just like Buddha and Dudley, but it is very clear to everyone else around us that he and I have a special relationship. He moos when he hears my voice, runs to the fence when he sees me, and seems to understand every word I say. This led me to start wondering more about reincarnation. Is John Lewis really Buddha? Is he Dudley? Is he the same soul that keeps coming back to me, over and over again? Is it possible that Buddha came to raise me and start the Gentle Barn, Dudley came to partner with me and bring the Gentle Barn national, and John Lewis came to be my baby, ushering me into my role as matriarch?

As an animal communicator, I have been learning a lot more about reincarnation. It comes up in readings. I start readings by first doing a quiet meditation to clear my thoughts. I check in with my own body so that I recognize what my aches and pains might be that day and don't interpret them as what the animal feels. Then I ask the animal questions. In one session I was talking to a beautiful, striking, very masculine

German shepherd who had passed away. He kept showing me an image of a German shepherd lying dead on a kitchen floor. He showed it over and over again. He showed me people walking into the kitchen in the morning and finding the animal dead on the kitchen floor.

When I relayed this to my clients, they acknowledged that years ago, they had a female German shepherd who they found dead on the kitchen floor. The male shepherd was not yet born when the female was their family dog. Out of curiosity, I asked to communicate with the female German shepherd as well. She showed me how the male German shepherd had passed away at the vet's office with the family around him. I had to wonder whether the male and female dogs were the same soul that came to these people twice? Why else would they know so much about each other?

Even though I was raised in an Orthodox Jewish household, from the time I was very small, I would pretend to be Native American without having learned anything about their cultures. It was something inside of me. Maybe an awareness of a past life? It seems obvious that we are somewhere before we incarnate in our bodies, and once we transition, there is somewhere that we go afterward. From speaking to hundreds of animals who have passed away, I have been told over and over again that animals stay connected to their loved ones and nothing can interrupt that connection. Love is unbreakable.

So what about us humans? Do we carry lessons forward from one lifetime to another? Do we stay connected after we leave our bodies?

Western cultures support the thought that we go somewhere when we die. Most people refer to "going to heaven" or "crossing over the rainbow bridge." Or we consider death to be the final ending, with only a void left where you once existed. What I'm hearing from animals who have died, though, is that they didn't go anywhere, except to leave their bodies behind. They prove to me that they still are very much engaged, connected, and in love with the people who loved them when they had bodies. They show me what their people are doing, they share favorite songs or phrases that their people still say to them, and they relay wishes for their people, like encouraging them to get another animal or take a trip. I think about reincarnation every time I hang out with John Lewis because being with him makes me feel like I am with Buddha and Dudley all over again.

While our Gentle Barn locations were closed during the first twenty months of the pandemic, our animals took the extra time to meditate longer, spend more time with each other, and enjoy having the barnyards to themselves. As time passed, though, most became surprisingly restless, missing the affection of our guests and the purpose of our programs. Once the CDC loosened the guidelines and we were able to reopen to the public, it was extraordinary to witness the warmth and smiling connections between each visitor and animal.

After seeing how effective the Cow Hug Therapy sessions were with Mandy and knowing thousands of people in our own community were in crisis and recovery from the pandemic, we expanded the program to make the sessions available to anyone. If someone was suffering from anxiety, depression, suicidal ideation, terminal illness, grief, despair, loss, or loneliness, or they just needed a good hug, they could come to the Gentle Barn and have their very own individual Cow Hug Therapy session.

It was incredible to watch our cows give out healings. They lay down, closed their eyes, held still, and helped people wash away the pandemic. They allowed people to cry onto their shoulders, and they formed circles around those who needed them most.

I noticed right away that John Lewis would act annoyed if people wanted to pet him just because he's cute or wanted to be entertained by him. He would walk away from their energy if it seemed like pointless curiosity or only interest in a photo opportunity. And sure enough, within a month of our reopening, John Lewis joined in and became the youngest member of our Cow Hug Therapy team. Intuitive, wise, and enlightened, he always made himself available to people who were truly suffering. He is here for real work, real healing, and real transformation for anyone who needs him.

Some people hug every single one of our cows and want to know each of their stories. Some gravitate to one particular cow and spend the entire hour with them.

When Emily arrived for her Cow Hug Therapy session, she didn't say why she was there, and I didn't pry. John Lewis was already lying down, so we approached him first. She knelt down beside him, leaned her body against him, rested her cheek on his shoulder, and closed her eyes. Lewis wrapped his neck around her and held her. It was so unexpected that this woman started weeping. Lewis held her for the entire session.

When the hour was over, I walked her to her car and she shared that her grandmother had just passed away, and she was really having a hard time. She didn't know what to do with her grief. She said that the way that Lewis got her to rid her mind of thought and just be present with him was exactly what she needed. She said that she didn't know how to explain it, and didn't know exactly why, but she felt much better. She felt like her grandmother was there in Lewis's embrace.

Kimberly came for a Cow Hug Therapy session around the same time. She had tears in her eyes already when she got out of her car. I walked her into the cow pasture just as John Lewis was lying down and closing his eyes. I invited her to kneel down and put her head on his shoulder. The moment Lewis wrapped his neck around her, the woman began to sob. Lewis held perfectly still for her. When she was done crying, she looked up at me and told me about her cancer diagnosis at the start of the pandemic. She had gone into the hospital for massive surgery and because of Covid, had to go through the surgery and weeks of recovery alone, without any family or friends by her side.

It's so scary to have a diagnosis like that, and even scarier to have such a major surgery. Can you imagine doing it alone? The woman described how the nurses had to wear hazmat suits with masks and gloves and couldn't even nurture her or give her a simple hug. The only thing she had as company was her phone. Trying to distract herself and find something to hold on to, she found the Gentle Barn social media accounts and started following John Lewis's rescue and recovery in our house. Watching videos and live streams of Lewis's illness, struggle, and revival gave her something to hope for. She reasoned that if our little orphaned calf could make it, then she could make it too, and she promised herself that when she was well, she would come meet John Lewis.

That very day, as Kimberly drove to the Gentle Barn to meet Lewis, her oncologist had called to give her the news that she was cancer free and in remission. In Lewis's embrace, Kimberly's were happy tears, letting go of the past year, the trauma, the loneliness, and the fear. With those tears she thanked John Lewis for being her North Star and guiding her through her own journey and celebrated with him that she would live.

A husband and wife came for a Cow Hug Therapy session after losing a nephew in a tragic car crash. Feeling devastated and lost along with the rest of their family, they thought the peacefulness of the Gentle Barn could help. Rachel was having an exceptionally hard time processing her grief. She had a large, bright personality, with a tough exterior that hid her real feelings. She talked a mile a minute, moved very quickly, had a lot of energy, and did not know how to connect with or process her grief at all.

In stark contrast with the cows' giant, grounded, still, and quiet energy, this grief-stricken woman found it impossible to sit still and give in to the cows' therapeutic presence. One of the wonderful things about cows is that no matter how somebody shows up, whether they have a disability with jerky movements, whether they're in a wheelchair or a stroller, whether they're depressed or anxious, the cows don't change their behavior or demeanor; they just hold steady to who and how they are.

Madonna is one of our largest cows. She is black and white with a massive frame and gentle energy. As Rachel kept talking nonstop, gesticulating with her hands, and moving all over the place, Madonna held still. Her eyes were closed, her face was pointing directly ahead, and her mouth was rhythmically chewing her cud. She didn't even swish her tail. She was offering this woman a safe space to land and find herself.

I brought Rachel over to Madonna, and as she was talking, I would quietly nod, encouraging her to relax and be silent. Over the next few minutes, her rattled speech slowed down, her arms rested on her lap, her facial expressions softened, and she started to come to a centered place. I asked her to please rest her body on Madonna's giant frame and put her face against Madonna's soft and fuzzy side.

Every now and then Rachel would tilt her head up and start talking again, but I would just gently encourage her to put her face back on Madonna and close her eyes. She finally found that sweet spot of surrender that all of our guests eventually find in Cow Hug Therapy, where thoughts vanish from the mind and the motions vanish from the body. She dropped away from doing, thinking, and moving and into vulnerability, openness, and being fully present.

After about fifteen minutes of resting against Madonna, Rachel moved in front of her and lay on the ground underneath Madonna's head. She just stayed there, head resting on the ground, hair tossed in the sand, arms extended out to each side, legs splayed out, eyes closed, and a soft expression on her face for the first time. She gave herself to Madonna, to Mother Earth beneath her, and to Father Sky above her. She fully surrendered. Her husband whispered in my ear that this was the first time he had seen her still and quiet in years.

When the session ended, the woman I said goodbye to was completely different from the one I had met an hour before. She seemed connected to her real feelings instead of deflecting, avoiding, or defending. She was present, grounded, authentic, and beautiful.

I had taken pictures of Rachel during the sessions and gave them to her to take home. I suggested that whenever she felt herself getting loud and agitated, she could look at the pictures of herself at the Gentle Barn with our cows, close her eyes for a few minutes, breathe in and out a few times, and bring back the feeling of being with Madonna. The memory would help her return to being still, quiet, present, and grounded wherever she was.

Being out in nature, in the fresh air, with animals is undeniably restorative by itself, but there are some deeper reasons, I believe, that Cow Hug Therapy is so important. When we're born, we're held on our parent's chest. We can hear their heartbeat, the rhythm of their breathing, and we feel safe even though we're small, helpless, and vulnerable. When we grow up, there is nothing that simulates that experience, except for hugging a cow. We can hug our partners, friends, or other animals, but that does not give us the same small and safe feeling.

When our tiny bodies lean against giant cows and we put our faces on them and close our eyes, we can hear their heartbeat, and it slows down our own. We can hear their breathing and connect to it. In that warm embrace, we feel safe, tiny, cared for, and open, and that is where healing starts. In that intuitive, right-brained vulnerability and connection without words, we can ground, center, be still, be quiet, and grow into infinite possibilities, just like an infant.

Anyone, no matter what they've gone through, no matter what they're feeling, can come for a Cow Hug Therapy session and find something that can only be found in a silent, warm, present-time embrace from a gentle giant generously holding still for us.

I needed that for myself too, especially as I faced my own aging and mortality, as so many of us did during the pandemic. When I was younger, in my teens and twenties, even my thirties, I was considered physically beautiful by others. At the time, though, I didn't see myself that way at all — I thought I was overweight and unattractive. I wasted all those precious years with a young, vibrant body, a beautiful face, healthy hair, and glowing skin because I couldn't appreciate what I was given. I focused only on what I saw as flaws.

Now, decades later, I see photos from my youth and can't remember why I had reason to complain. It is ironic: now that I have done so much work on myself, healing and finding out who I am, I'm actually comfortable with myself, even though I am older and my body weighs more than it ever has before. I try to remember that in a decade or so, I will look back at pictures from now and see myself as beautiful, the same way I do now with pictures from my twenties. I might as well not waste any more time seeing myself as anything less than beautiful.

The pandemic gave many of us time to look at ourselves and perceive, hopefully in a gentle and accepting way, how we had been spending our time and living our lives. We were given time for introspection about where we were at and whether we were happy in our current circumstances. Many people began to take the first steps on a different path for themselves. With or without a cow to hug, we received from the pandemic the grace to center our souls, prioritize what was most important, draw us closer to our true purpose, and align in a way that can bring more peace and happiness going forward.

CHAPTER TWELVE

WHISPER

All is forgiven. It is all right to bid farewell to the past
and accept mistakes as lessons learned.

— WHISPER

When I married my first husband, Scott, I was in my twenties, and I hoped to be in a lifelong relationship with someone who loved and understood me for who I was. For a few years Scott did his best to be that person for me. I wanted to be that person for him too.

Scott's parents had given us a generous amount of money to use on our honeymoon. As we settled in after the wedding, I saw a photo of two baby horses in a magazine published in Southern California. The article stated that the babies, who lived on a farm about twenty-five miles from us, would soon need a home. I was drawn to them, but I put the magazine away, feeling it was too much to ask. And then I got it back out, again and again. I thought about those little horses every day.

When Scott brought up how to use the money given us for our honeymoon, I showed him the photo of the two horses. I proposed an idea that made perfect sense to me: A fabulous honeymoon would be over in a week, but these horses would be with us for years. They'd be part of our family. I explained that we could use the money to fix up the little barn we had on our property and also have enough to bring the fillies home when they were old enough.

Scott paused for a moment, but he could see on my face that it was all I really wanted. A horse of my own was something I had longed for since I could first pronounce the word *horse*. I spent my childhood collecting Breyer horse figurines, in every size, color, and breed that was made. I played with them for hours, while my dolls lay on a shelf untouched.

When I was finally old enough to ask, my parents enrolled me in riding lessons after school. I would beg them for a horse of my own, but they never saw it as necessary or practical. Still, I would dream of having a horse.

As I got a little older, to placate my unrelenting passion, my parents would send me to a horseback riding camp for a couple of weeks during the summer and allow me to go to a stable for a trail ride on Sundays. When riding, I held my head up, shoulders back, heels pointed down, my body in perfect rhythm with the horse's. Perfect posture had been formed in my body memory thanks to my excellent teachers, who taught me to ride with confidence and to listen to my instincts.

It made no difference whether I was cleaning up after them, walking them, grooming them, riding them, or just watching them eat, everything about horses was magical to me. I knew that one day I would have a horse of my own, no matter what. This seemed like the exact right opportunity to make my dream come true.

Eager to make me happy, Scott agreed. We visited the fillies every day. I couldn't wait to see them. I would bite my nails down to nubs waiting for Scott to get home from work. After a quick bite to eat, we would jump into his big open Jeep, strap ourselves in, and drive the forty-five minutes it took to see our horses. We named them Willow and Whisper.

Willow was only six weeks old but already tall for her age. She was a bay, with a smooth brown body and black mane and tail. She had long, strong legs, a very pretty face, a little brown nubby tail and mane, and huge cartoon character eyes. She was sweet, humble, and innocent, and I just wanted to protect her forever.

Whisper was only four weeks old, with a mousy gray body that would later turn jet-black, and fluff where her mane and tail were supposed to be. Right from the start, Whisper was smart, curious, a little mischievous, and full of energy, with permanent sparkles in her eyes. Her legs were long and thin, and she looked just like the Breyer horse figurines from my childhood.

We spent hours petting them, bonding with them, getting them used to the halter and lead rope, walking them around, and becoming a family. Only when the sun went down would Scott and I head for home.

When the horses were four months old, we were told that it was time for them to come to our place. I had never raised baby horses before, but I had a strong feeling that they were still too young and needed their moms. The farm owners who had them reassured us that they were ready and insisted that we either take them home or give them to someone else. I offered to pay board so they could stay with their moms longer, but when they refused, I gave up and agreed to take them home. In those days, I gave my authority to other people. I saw everyone else as the expert and ignored my instincts in the face of argument.

We all have regrets that we accumulate, collect, and carry with us. Taking those baby horses away from their moms is a regret I will take with me to the grave. Everything inside me was saying that it was wrong, but the people would not have it any other way. I didn't want the horses to be given to someone else after I had become so attached, and I didn't know then how to stand in my own certainty.

Their homecoming was supposed to be sweet and full of joy, a childhood dream come true. We had our barn ready with soft bedding, fresh hay, and clean water. We had a barnyard that they could gallop around and play in. I even planned on leaving our bedroom windows open all night so that I could hear them out in the barn if they needed me.

But there was no galloping or playing those first few months. Whisper and Willow just stood there with their heads hung low, in shock and despair. I called and asked the farm owners if I could bring their moms to our property as well. They said no.

I would end up spending the nights in the barnyard, holding the horses' heads in my lap, apologizing to them over and over again for the pain they were in. I had participated in hurting these two horses because I wanted them so badly, and it broke me to know they were unhappy.

Time passed and ushered the four of us forward. Eventually Willow and Whisper found joy in the backyard and on the walks we would take with them every evening. Scott and I made their lives as perfect as possible, cleaning their barn until it was spotless and grooming them until their coats shined.

When the honeymoon phase of our marriage ended, so did Scott's interest in Willow and Whisper. Our son Jesse was born after our first year, and Scott became absorbed in financial woes and work obligations. I found myself alone with a nursing newborn and two yearlings who were growing bigger by the day. Walking two young horses by myself through the neighborhood and on the nearby trails was really challenging, but the less I would walk them, the harder it became. They were young and full of pent-up energy.

By their second birthday they started testing me. They considered me a member of the herd and began jockeying for a power position, kicking or nipping at me to see how I would respond. To teach them to behave within clear constraints while making sure they still felt safe, I needed to be a strong parent with strong boundaries. I failed to do that.

My whole life I had wanted my own horse to love, care for, and be with. I didn't realize that I also had to discipline them. I started letting them push me around and bully me. Each time I failed to be strong, their bad behavior got worse. By the time they were about three years old, I dreaded having to handle them at all. I even interpreted their bad behavior as meaning they hated me, and I didn't know what to do. I was in over my head and needed help!

I had heard about a trainer from Colorado, Mark Rashid, who had worked with wild horses and practiced natural horsemanship. He learned from the wild mustangs that every herd has a matriarch who decides where and when to eat, drink, and sleep. She brings the family together and makes them feel safe and organized. Her mate helps her discipline the others, settle disputes, and protect the family from invading herds. By controlling the movement of the other horses, this lead stallion shows them who's boss and ensures that they submit to him. Mark adapted this model, training horses in a gentle way. He was rumored to be the best horse whisperer of all time.

Whisper was harder for me to handle than Willow, so Mark chose to work with her first. In a round pen, he began moving Whisper around in easy circles. In the first session, her ears, eyes, and face were pointed outside the circle, to ignore and avoid Mark's directions. He then began changing where he asked her to go, sending her in wider and wider circles under his control, and sending the message to Whisper, without force or intimidation, that he was the leader. Soon he had Whisper's attention, and she flexed one ear toward him, listening. She shifted her neck to the inner side of the circle instead of defiantly turning away. After about fifteen minutes or so, Mark stood still and silent. Whisper stopped moving and turned toward him. He bowed his head, and Whisper walked all the way to him at the center of the circle and nuzzled his outstretched hand with her velveteen nose.

Mark then gave her a break and came to where I stood at

the fence to talk with me. He reassured me that Whisper was not a vicious or bad-tempered horse who had grown to hate me; she was only a young girl who needed the security of a strong mom.

I hadn't the faintest idea how to be a strong mom. All my life I had been directed to be a nice person, behave in a humble way, stay within the rules, and be smart. No one ever told me my opinions mattered or that having a fierce and strong backbone and healthy self-esteem would serve me when it came to being a leader. I only knew how to follow other people's opinions and go with their advice. I knew that the expert in the room was never me. How could I be a strong mom now?

Mark brought me into the middle of the round pen and worked with Whisper and me, showing me how to move her around. He showed me how to use my eyes and intention: if I looked at her shoulder, my gaze would encourage her to keep going, but if I looked at her hind legs, it would move her hind end away from me and ask her to face me. He taught me how to use my body language to communicate with her and how to interpret her body language when she was communicating with me. When she was running around the circle and her ears were pointed to the outside of the round pen, she was blowing me off. He showed me how to get her attention back on me. Once Whisper was fully engaged with me, he showed me how to stop, then join up with her in the middle of the circle, reaching my hand out to stroke her face and neck. For the first time in a long time, I felt like we were family again.

We had made tremendous progress, and I didn't want it to backslide when Mark left. Mark had a student, Stacy, who had spent time training with him on his ranch in Colorado. Stacy offered to board Whisper and Willow at her place and help me gain confidence to fully heal our relationship and raise the girls properly. We moved both horses into her stable, a beautiful setup with a warm barn and spacious pasture. Stacy lived on the property and could see and hear the horses from her house.

I drove to Stacy's house several times a week. We always started by grooming the girls: using the currycomb, a flatter brush made of rubber, to massage their necks and backs in tight little circles; then using a softer brush to brush their whole bodies of dirt and dead hair, brushing out their manes and tails; then cleaning out their hooves and washing their faces with a warm washcloth, cleaning their eyes, nostrils, and mouths. Most horses don't like their faces cleaned, but for some reason Whisper always loved it, leaning into it and allowing us to clean right up into her nose.

One day Stacy's next-door neighbor came over for a visit and met my horses. She had been looking for a horse of her own for quite some time and fell head over heels in love with Willow. I knew that Willow and Whisper would get way more attention if they each had a person of their own, and Scott was disconnected from the whole idea of horse care, so it seemed a great solution. Her land was right next door, where Willow and Whisper could still see each other, and I could keep an eye on Willow and make sure it was a good fit for her. The neighbor came to spend time with Willow every day for a while, and once they had bonded, Willow moved next door to have all the attention she desired. Willow loved her new mom and lived with her happily ever after, for the rest of her life.

Stacy's neighborhood was the perfect place to have a horse. Right in front of her property were many riding trails that wound their way through streams and over mountains. There were miles of orange orchards to either side, and once in a while, I would pick and peel open a fresh orange and feed it to Whisper, who munched happily with juice trickling down her chin. There was a fenced five acres where we could let Whisper off the lead rope and let her gallop around, explore, and graze while Stacy and I rested under giant pepper trees and talked.

Stacy and I got to know each other well and bonded like sisters. She told me about her marriage, and I shared things about mine. With our shared love of horses, not only did we enjoy our time together but she helped me mend my relationship with Whisper. Over time and with patience, I stepped up as a strong mom, and Whisper settled down into a sweet, good girl. We were connected. This was what I had been dreaming of my entire life, and it was heaven.

When Jesse was an early toddler, I would bring along a mommy's helper, and the two of them could play for an hour or two while I was with Stacy and Whisper. As Jesse got a little older, he didn't want to just wander around Stacy's yard. He wanted to play with his own toys and be creative on his own, without the restrictions of getting in a car and going to someone else's house. Caring for Jesse and Whisper at the same time created a constant feeling of being torn down the middle. When I took the time to be with Whisper, Jesse would cry or be angry. When I stayed home to be with Jesse, I felt guilty about Whisper.

Watching me struggle, Stacy and Mark told me about someone they knew and trusted who lived up in Northern California and was looking for a horse. They said Ed practiced natural horsemanship and was confident, quiet, and kind. He had a gorgeous and green twenty acres with other horses to offer Whisper companionship, and I could focus on being with my son. I agreed that Ed should meet Whisper, and from the start it seemed to be a good match. He was charmed by Whisper, and she seemed to enjoy and trust him as well.

I knew that any decision I made was going to bring some guilt. I spent countless nights walking the floor, trying to meditate on the right thing to do and then crying over my own feelings of failing Whisper. I finally concluded that the closest thing to a win-win situation for all of us was if Whisper went on an adventure and got the care she needed, while I focused on Jesse and gave him the care he needed.

When the time came, I covered Whisper in kisses and told her that I loved her with all my heart. I promised her that if anything was ever wrong, that if she needed me, that if she wasn't happy anymore, I would come and get her. I had drawn up a contract for Ed to sign, stating that he wouldn't sell her or give her away, would stay in touch with me, and if something wasn't right, he would return her to me. Whisper got up into the trailer without hesitation and without looking back.

After that, as I was taking Jesse to the park, baby music classes, and indoor playgrounds, I kept in touch with Ed and thought about Whisper all the time. All the news coming from them was great. She was bonding with the other horses, eating lush grass, enjoying slow rides on the trails, and luxuriating in the attention of her new man. Every time I thought of her, I felt a happy feeling come back to me.

Several months later, however, I felt a concerned feeling coming from her. I called Ed right away and asked if there was something wrong. Ed said, "I can't believe you're calling. This is uncanny. Wow, you really have a close relationship with her."

He explained to me that she had accidentally tripped and was a little lame. The vet came out and took a look. "She's just a little bit sore," he said.

He continued, "But I can't believe you picked that up. Anyway, don't worry about her. She's going to be on stall rest, and she'll be fine in a few days."

Sure enough, a few days later when I thought of her, happy, peaceful feelings came back to me. It was reassuring that I could feel her, know how she was doing, and would know if she ever needed me.

For the next several years Whisper thrived. I knew she was happy because I could feel it, but I also called Ed to make sure. Each phone call gave me a positive report that they were both doing well. Ed would tell me all about their trail rides and fun, and I would tell Ed about my eventual divorce with Scott, how my son was growing and becoming a fantastic boy, and years later, about meeting Jay and the opening of the Gentle Barn.

When Jay and I fell in love and got married, I would talk to him about Whisper often. Jay knew all about her. I showed him pictures and told him stories about her. I remember telling Jay that even though Whisper was happy with Ed, for some unexplainable reason I knew deep in my soul that one day I was going to get her back. I felt like she was a part of me and that we were soulmates. For whatever reason, we were meant to be apart now, but she was going to come back to me one day.

Thanks to Ed, I had six years to focus on Jesse. We played together and did the things he wanted to do, like T-ball, play-dates with his friends, trips to the beach, visits to museums, and lots of slow, uninterrupted time to give him my full attention. We both welcomed Jay into our lives along with his daughter Molli, whom I would nurture and raise.

About six years later, I was eight months pregnant with our daughter Cheyanne when all of a sudden I woke up in the middle of the night with an awful feeling about Whisper. I thought about her all the next morning and knew that there was something terribly, terribly wrong. I called Ed, and while the phone was ringing, I had such an anxious feeling in my stomach that when Ed finally answered I blurted out a little too loud, "What is wrong with Whisper?!"

Ed explained that he had hurt his back and hadn't been able to spend time with her. Not wanting to bother me, he had given her away to a neighbor who needed a horse to help him with his cattle.

I exploded. "How could you do that? You signed a contract saying that she would come back to me! You promised me!"

"Look," he said, "it's been many years. She's been so happy. This guy just lives down the street. I thought, what's the harm? She could be ridden and have a job, and my back could mend. I didn't want to bother you."

I was not appeased. "Whisper is in trouble, and I must have her back!"

Jay came into the room just as I was hanging up. I was crying so hard I could barely get the words out, but I managed to tell him about Whisper and what had happened. He didn't respond right away. He stared at the ground for a few minutes, his eyes moving side to side. I could see he was figuring out a way to make this right.

Having never seen this horse and without any emotional attachment to her, my husband, who had a million things to do that day, nonetheless dropped them all in selfless love for me. He looked up and said, "I'm going to get her."

Jay went upstairs and packed a small bag, hooked up the trailer to our truck, gave me a kiss goodbye, and drove the ten hours up to Northern California, bringing the signed adoption contract with him. When Jay arrived, he told Ed's neighbor, the man who had Whisper, that he was there to bring her home. He was not leaving without her and would stay as long as it took. Jay told Ed's neighbor that he could do it the easy way and release Whisper to him today, or he would get the police involved. The man just squinted his eyes at Jay, about to shut the door.

Then Jay held up the contract. "Look. I have a legally signed document. Whisper belongs to my wife, and Ed had no right to give her to you. So I'm not leaving without the horse."

Then he stood there, nonthreatening but firm. The man argued and refused, wavered and negotiated, but Jay stood there with the contract. Hours later, it appeared the man had closed himself up in his house. Jay took a seat in his truck, counting on it being a chilly and damp night. A thick layer of fog rolled in, making it impossible to see more than fifteen yards.

As Jay was about to call me to say he would be spending the night in his truck, he looked in the sideview mirror and saw the figure of a horse emerging through the thick fog. He jumped out to see Whisper standing in front of him, her lead rope held by Ed's angry neighbor. Jay took the rope, and the man, realizing what he was up against, released his grip, turned, and walked away.

Jay was finally standing in front of a horse he had heard about for years, who was as much a part of me as my hands and feet. He intended on spending a minute getting to know her, but Whisper just wanted to get out of there and walked herself onto the trailer. Jay respected her urgency and got them on the road, headed for home.

While Jay drove, I fed Jesse and Molli dinner, got them in the bath, and put them to bed. Then I waited anxiously for Jay and Whisper to arrive. I must have dozed off and was awakened by Jay's call that they were home. I ran downstairs barefoot, in my pajamas, flung open the front door, and there was Jay and my Whisper standing side by side in the front yard.

Whisper and I had a signature thing that we had done with each other ever since the day we met. Every time we greeted each other, she would reach out her neck toward me and extend her face to mine until her nose was right in front of mine. We would breathe each other in, and I would kiss her soft lips. Seeing each other for the first time in six years, I did not know if she would be angry at me or if she had forgotten about me. As soon as I was standing in front of her, though, Whisper reached out her neck and face toward me, put her lips against mine, and I closed my eyes while we breathed each other in. To this day, I can still recall the smell of her sweet nostrils blowing into mine. I have heard movies and stories depict angels as smelling like cookies, but I disagree. I think an angel would smell like a horse's muzzle.

In the light of the next morning, I was able to see the extent of the damage to Whisper's body and spirit. She had cigar burns on her rear and holes on either side of her body from being kicked with spurs, her chest was rubbed raw from the saddle strap, her hooves were too long, causing tendon damage, and her fury at how she had been treated was oozing out of her.

I asked her gently to back up so I could open the door to her stall, and the request pushed her into a violent, seething rage, rearing, kicking, and throwing her feet behind her. I felt responsible and sick to my stomach for the way she had been abused, and she had every right to tell me all about it. In a desperate attempt to show her I was listening, I walked into the middle of her stall, closed my eyes, hung my head to show her that I posed no threat, and stood my ground. Whisper raced around me and at me, ears back, teeth bared, and feet kicking. I could feel the air brush my skin as she passed by me, inches from my body.

Jay, realizing where I had gone, ran to the stable door, saying, "Ellie, get out of there! You are not safe! Don't be crazy. She could hurt you." But I stayed, knowing that the only way I could get her trust back was if I first gave my trust to her.

Whisper made all kinds of threats that day, but she never actually made contact with me or hurt me in any way. I knew that was not coincidental, but deliberate. Whisper did not want to hurt me — she loved me. She did, however, want to show me how angry, hurt, and scared she was. After a while, she stopped raging and walked over to me, put her mouth on mine, and exhaled a long, loud breath, letting a little bit of her agony go.

I kept repeating, "I am so very sorry, I am so sorry, please forgive me!" Animals do not typically tend to hold grudges, and by the end of the day it seemed that Whisper had already forgiven me. It would take me the rest of her lifetime, however, to forgive myself.

Whisper's extensive physical wounds healed slowly while we introduced her to our other horses and integrated her into our equine family. Healing her emotional wounds would prove to be a much longer process.

Whisper's behavior and triggers made it clear that her abuser had punished her violently when she didn't respond immediately to his demands. Whisper had never met cows before, and she had never been trained as a cutting horse. He probably gave her commands and then beat her when she didn't do as he asked, not understanding his request. Whisper was now afraid of being asked to do anything, even things she knew how to do, for fear of being abused again.

We found a Los Angeles–based trainer named Gary Hardle. Like Mark Rashid, Gary was a natural horseman who learned all his training methods from watching wild mustangs. He came up with a plan that began by bringing Whisper back to the scene of the crime.

When we rescue an animal from trauma and just release them into a pasture to retire, that trauma lives on inside of them, possibly creating disease. When we take them back to the environment of their abuse, give them an opportunity to express their rage, sadness, and fear, see once and for all that it is over, and work through their trauma, they can permanently heal from it and let it go.

Gary sat quietly on Whisper and asked her to do little things that she knew how to do, like take a step forward, turn to the left or right, or back up. When he would make these small requests, Whisper would explode into a bucking, kicking, and rearing rage. Gary sat on her quietly without restraining or controlling her, allowing her to express herself completely. Gary came every week, and the more she raged, the more she got the anger out of her body, and the closer she got to having peace.

Whisper got to tell us with her body language what had happened to her. We kept encouraging her to tell us more. Each week Whisper became a tiny bit softer until finally, four years later, she had nothing left to tell. The anger was gone. She set her past down and walked away from it. She was free.

The very last time Gary came out to work with Whisper, we groomed her and led her out of the barn, but instead of riding her, I pulled everything off her and set her free. She stood there not exactly sure what was happening or what she should do. I told her that her recovery was complete and that she was done. I told her how proud of her I was and praised her for being so resilient, brave, strong, and honest. I promised her she would be mine for the rest of her life and that she would never be ridden again. I gestured toward the small patch of grass growing just outside our horse pasture, and she went to graze, happily swishing her tail. Gary and I were both beaming, we gave each other huge hugs, and Jay and I thanked him from the bottom of our hearts for helping Whisper.

Whisper always had a fantastic work ethic. She was professional, respectful, and eager to please. I think that is why her abuse was so painful, because had the man just asked her and shown her what to do, she would have been happy to oblige. With her newfound freedom at the Gentle Barn, Whisper found a new purpose and a different way to carry people.

After years of hosting, I had an understanding about teenagers who came to visit the Gentle Barn from drug and alcohol rehab centers, homeless shelters, and probation camps. I knew they had often been told, their whole young lives, to sit down, be quiet, and follow the rules. They felt they were left with one of two choices, to shut down or to act out. With their heads hung low, their limp handshakes, looking away from me, these young people reminded me of wilted flowers.

I understood it. They were protecting their vulnerable feelings. But underneath every defeated exterior I could find a survivor: each one resilient, strong, powerful, and intuitive. I knew the animals could help them find this out about themselves.

When these young people first stepped out of the cars and vans on the Gentle Barn property and saw me waiting for them, I could see on their faces that they saw me as merely one more adult authority figure, ready to give them orders and directions. I needed them to know that I was different, that I saw them, and that I was listening. Instead of talking to them about the Gentle Barn or what expectations I had of them while they were here, I decided to start our time together by telling them Whisper's story.

Whisper's story was their story. Whisper wasn't a bad horse, but rather a horse who was hurt, abandoned, betrayed, and abused, with every right to be angry. They also had been betrayed in one way or another, they were angry too, and it wasn't their fault. There was no way that Whisper could have found happiness while full of rage, she needed to express her anger first. When I told this part of her story, I would see a connection in their eyes, a possibility. Later, I would hear from their therapists and teachers that through Whisper's story, the teenagers began to open up to them, feel validated in their own anger, and begin the struggle to heal.

Decades later, on a Sunday at the Gentle Barn, a thirty-something woman came up to say hello and to ask if I recognized her. She had first come to the Gentle Barn fifteen years earlier, when she was still a teenager. As a girl, she feared that no one would ever understand what she had been through. She had been sex trafficked and was full of shame and secrecy, wondering constantly if it was somehow her fault. She had decided that she had no chance of a normal life and was just waiting for an opportunity and way to commit suicide.

At the Gentle Barn that day as a teen, when she met the animals and heard their stories, she realized that like her, they all had their own pasts. She saw that the animals' histories were no longer defining them and that they had friends, family, and good lives. She applied those thoughts to herself. Perhaps her own past didn't have to define her future. The animals at the Gentle Barn helped her do well in school, graduate with honors, go on to college, and even get married and have a family of her own. She told me that our animals helped her feel normal. And Whisper was her favorite.

Whisper and I were able to make up for lost time and fully reinstated our bond. I groomed her daily, was always present for veterinary, acupuncture, massage, or chiropractic appointments, and made sure my staff never disrespected her or treated her like an object. I trained them all to tell her what was happening, and why, before touching her. We would regularly walk on the hiking trails side by side, and once we passed the last house before the national forest, I would take her halter and lead rope off and let her run free. Whisper would stop to munch on grass while I kept walking and moments later, come galloping to catch up with me. If she heard a strange sound, she ran to me for protection. We rested under shade trees and ran up hills till we were both winded.

We trusted each other completely and breathed each other in every single morning. I had grown from a young, inexperienced mother who trusted everyone else but myself to the confident, intuitive, and centered mom that Whisper and my kids needed.

One morning, as the pandemic began to wind down and more people began resuming their regular lives, I went to the barnyard to give John Lewis a bottle and check on all the other animals. Whisper took her morning cookie happily and then sent me an unexpected message. She told me our time together was short and asked me to be with her now whenever I could. I heard her voice very clearly but had no idea what it meant, as she was very healthy at age twenty-five.

A few days later, I was doing my morning checks and found Whisper writhing in pain on her side. I could see that she was colicking. A colic can be caused by an intestinal blockage, a twist of the intestines, tumors, stones, or even gas. Sometimes it is fatal and sometimes it is not, but it is always extremely painful.

Whisper was sweating over her entire body and breathing hard as Jay and I raced to put her into the trailer and drive her to the equine hospital, arriving in a record-breaking forty-five minutes. The veterinarians rushed out to our trailer to meet us. We walked her inside to stand in the stanchions so they could examine her. X-rays, ultrasound, and blood work showed that she had a blockage of unknown origin that was causing her gut to be impacted, and her intestines had begun to decay. The surgeon asked if Whisper was a surgical candidate and warned that we didn't have much time to decide. Normally sending a senior horse into surgery is very risky and a big deal, but Whisper was in such outstanding health that Jay and I asked for the surgery without hesitation.

While Jay and I watched from the upstairs viewing room, the equine surgeon and his team brilliantly sedated, sterilized, and opened up my Whisper to find three huge tumors. They

removed the tumors and with them, seventeen feet of intestines. Several hours later, a wobbly Whisper walked out of the
surgical suite and was led to her recovery stall. She was set up
with intravenous fluids, antibiotics, pain medication, and a
nurse who would take her vitals throughout the night. I was
not leaving her side.

For two months Whisper fought to get better as I sang
to her, read to her, brushed her, kissed and hugged her, and
cheered her on. I bought a brand-new pink groom kit with a
soft, shiny brush that would be hers alone. I had a bag of soft,
chewy molasses and oat cookies to feed her once she was feeling better. I got to know the other patients and their people. I
was on a first-name basis with the staff and was always there for
morning and evening rounds so I could hear the latest update
on my girl's condition.

When Whisper was finally cleared to eat solid food and
leave her stall, we would go for long, slow walks between the
lemon and avocado orchards that surrounded the hospital. We
stood under the shade of giant eucalyptus trees that danced in
the breeze coming off the ocean just thirty minutes away. She
ate grass, swatted at flies, and watched the comings and goings
of the other horses, people, trailers, and veterinarians. Horses
came and went daily, but there were other horses who, like
Whisper, were there for the long haul, with injuries, illnesses,
and surgeries to recover from. Whisper and the other horses
bonded and formed a little hospital family, who whinnied their
greetings as we came and went on our walks.

We moved forward with a very guarded prognosis. While
Whisper munched grass on our walks, I would stare at her, trying to commit to memory the way her little ears curved inward
at the tops; her giant eyes, and how the bottom lids drooped
down when she got worried about something; her velvet black
coat that I loved to bury my face in; her round, sexy butt,

which she used to back up to people on open Sundays and ask them to scratch; the white star on her forehead, the blaze down her face, and the pink snip on her nose that I loved to kiss; and of course the warm hay and honey scent of her breath as I breathed her in.

After rallying and putting up a strong fight for many weeks, Whisper began to colic again, this time rolling on the ground of her hospital room repeatedly in agony. We were without a surgical option this time; she would never survive it. The doctors spent hours trying every treatment and medication they could think of, to no avail. The rolling and the pain were only intensifying.

At nightfall the veterinarian came to me with tears in his eyes and said he was out of options — the intestines were clearly dying off, and she was suffering. We needed to help her out of her body. Moments before the doctor had approached us, Whisper had stopped in mid roll, looked up at me, and asked me imploringly to help her. She was asking for relief, for help, for mercy. My only answer back to the doctor was, "She is ready."

I knew in my heart that Whisper had already told me she was going to pass away, before anything happened, and I now believe that she stuck around not to recover but to give us time to hide away in this hospital together. She was given my full love and attention because I was away from work, family, responsibilities, and other animals. Without anyone else around, I came to trust her and my own instincts, and the deep soulmate bond that the two of us were always meant to share. We had come full circle, and in the center of it was forgiveness and healing.

I walked Whisper home without fear. Thanks to all that our cows had taught me about transition, I knew with every fiber of my soul that she was leaving her body but not leaving me. Closing my eyes, I could feel her spirit lift out of her body and envelop mine. I could feel her all around me, and I still do, to this day. She visits me in my dreams, comes to me in my thoughts every day. She will always be a part of me.

In my time with Whisper, I made mistakes and was forgiven. I was weak but found strength. I was scared and found reassurance. I went from an insecure people pleaser to a mom, founder, and leader. When I was with horses as a child, I felt invincible, confident, and powerful. Whisper brought that feeling back to me and left it with me, returning to me a piece of myself that made me whole once more.

CHAPTER THIRTEEN

MATRIARCH

Know who you are and what you want, and never back down.
You are always right.

— MENORAH

Matriarch animals lead horizontally, unlike patriarchs, who usually put down the rule of law like a vertical post, not to be questioned. A matriarch animal is revered in her family because she leads in a way that serves the entire group, leaving nothing and no one unnoticed. A matriarch has collected insight and knowledge from the experiences she has gone through, and she stands in unapologetic confidence, knowing how to guide her family members.

Buddha was my first mother figure at the Gentle Barn. She perceived my need for a comforting shoulder on which to lean when I was being tested, and she supported my dream of the Gentle Barn. She created Cow Hug Therapy specifically for me, treating me as a vulnerable member of her family. She allowed me to weep into her coat, spill all my concerns, and be consoled by her warm, protective hugs. And she didn't let me stay there. She brought forward my resilience, even when I doubted it in myself, and when I was stronger, she insisted that I sit beside her and learn to meditate instead of collapsing into her strength. She wasn't rejecting me in this; she was expecting me to rise up into my own sense of self.

After Buddha left her body, I remained in the care of loving matriarch animals. These were always the cows who arrived to help me with my mission. Buddha passed her torch to Buttercup, Buttercup passed it to Karma, Karma passed it to Crystal, and Crystal passed her knowledge to Holy Cow, our current bovine leader. Matriarchs don't just leave. They feel themselves getting older and they train the next matriarch.

The other matriarchs who have guided and nurtured me most included Whisper, my beloved horse, and my companion dog, Socks. Whisper helped me gain my confidence, and Socks always mirrored to me that I was lovable, no matter how I perceived my shortcomings.

During the three years of the pandemic, Karma, Socks, and Whisper all took their leave from my life, and for the first time I was alone, without a longtime matriarch to mother me when I needed guidance. Of course, I was surrounded by cherished loved ones who I took care of, but my mother figures, the ones who took care of me, were no longer in my barnyard.

Walking down the path one day to give the cows and horses their bedtime cookies, I wondered why all three of my trusted matriarchs had left me in such a short period of time. As I looked at John Lewis, the baby cow I had kept alive through sheer will and nonstop nurturing, now standing strong and full of life force, the answer came to me: *I* was to be the new matriarch.

It was my turn to step up. I needed to collect the many lessons I had learned, stabilize them with my confidence, and guide my children, my animals, and the community of the Gentle Barn into a future that would serve all — from the abandoned lamb to the defeated donkey to the lonely foster children to the enthusiastic volunteers to the grieving, heartbroken, and forgotten, whether animal or human. I needed to fully drop the message I had told myself in my twenties, that I didn't know how to be a strong mommy, and become the pillar of resource, care, and guidance for my two grown children and my teen daughter.

I began to assess where I was on my path to becoming a matriarch and exactly what needed to change to embrace my role fully. When you ask to be shown what you need to learn, sometimes the lessons come fast and with purpose.

When Jay and I ran the Gentle Barn, making decisions together, I felt good and knew who I was. I was Jay Weiner's wife, the mother of his children, and founder of the Gentle Barn. We saved animals, healed them, and gave hope to people. That was my identity.

In the past, Jay and I normally traveled together, but now with three locations, our three children, two hundred animals, dozens of staff, and hundreds of volunteers to manage, a new arrangement was necessary. We had to divide and conquer.

Our relationship had also changed. The Gentle Barn now pulled Jay and me away from each other, to separate states, separate rooms, separate beds, and separate lives, and I found myself struggling. Even though Jay never gave me a reason to question his devotion to me, I found myself asking: Does he still love me? Am I still attractive? Does he think about me? Does he miss me?

One day Jay and I were driving Cheyanne to a photo shoot. I was staring dreamily out the car window, remembering back to when I was an actress, a million years ago. This was already making me feel my age when, at a red light, my husband looked over at me and casually said, "You know, you've got a really long hair there." I looked in the mirror with horror and saw a long, dark hair growing out of my neck. Embarrassed, I could feel my face flush bright red. I felt unattractive and old, and could only wonder what was happening to the rest of my body. I pulled the hair out of my neck and then couldn't even look Jay in the eye.

At this moment I realized that although I was already in my fifties, I still didn't have a secure concept of who I was. How could something so insignificant as a hair that needed to be plucked tip me off-balance so easily? Did my looks, my weight, and getting older matter so much to me that changes would forever make me feel insecure?

When the photo shoot was over and we were driving home, we stopped for a takeout lunch. As we were about to get back onto the freeway, we noticed on the on-ramp a homeless person asking for money and food. Without hesitation, without a thought, I handed over our newly acquired meal. As the man grew smaller and smaller in the rearview mirror, I could see him tearing open the bag, taking out the food, and eating it with much enthusiasm and appreciation, taking several big, juicy bites at a time. Tears sprung to my eyes as I thought to myself, "That's who I am. I am generous and thoughtful." All of a sudden, my neck hair seemed insignificant.

For years, I had told children and young people with challenges that their past, the mistakes they've made, how they look, and what other people said about them did not define them. I had told them that what defines us every single day is our actions, and I had shared with them the good news that when we don't like the actions of yesterday, we can always choose again today and redefine ourselves all over again. I had raised my own children to think for themselves and discover and honor who they were. But somehow, I had not applied these same principles to myself. I was judgmental about my own actions and insecure in my need for outside validation.

Once we were home, I went upstairs to change into my barnyard clothes and boots and took a long look at myself in the full-length mirror.

Yes, my once silky, straight black hair was now laced with some plain gray streaks. Yes, I had deeper wrinkles around my eyes and from the corners of my lips. My stomach wasn't flat anymore, and my thighs were wider than when I was a young woman. "Yes, that's true," I told myself.

I tried looking at myself as I would view a beloved friend. I knew I would say to her, "Your hair is gray because you have cared so much and felt deep concerns for the welfare of your family and the world, both people and animals. The lines now etched into your face are from smiling a million times and crying a thousand times because you are passionate about your hopes and dreams. Your stomach is no longer flat because you brought new life into the world through your children, and with age and the passage of time, nature gave you a softer body that also protects you. What you see as unattractive or something to hide, I see as battle scars and trophies earned through life experiences and wisdom gained."

I thought about my experiences and how what I learned from them did result in wisdom — wisdom that a matriarch can use to lead her family or group. I had gone through multiple suicide attempts and found a way to keep living. I had gone through drug addiction and found a way to stay clean. I'd gone through a failed marriage but found a way to love again. I had persevered and expanded the Gentle Barn through great challenges, I had opened my heart and soul to animals, family members, friends, and readers of my first book. Even though there were many times that Jay and I found ourselves in financial ruin or wanting to quit, we kept going. The Gentle Barn was now thriving in three locations.

I thought about all this, still looking at myself in the mirror, and told myself, "When I forget who I am, I can also look backward at all the things I've accomplished and the obstacles I have overcome, and in them, a lot of wisdom gained." I zipped up my Gentle Barn jacket, still musing. Then I said to my reflection in the mirror, "Ellie, you're the person who gives her lunch away to someone who needs it more. That's who you are."

I began to appreciate each step toward being a matriarch, even though it was something only I could do, for myself. I started paying very close attention to my actions, my values, my instincts, and how I showed up in the world. I took responsibility for my reactions to others, no matter how they were showing up or what was going on. I practiced taking responsibility for things without blaming anyone else. I paid attention to the way I felt inside, and I started feeling the foundation of pride in what was my own empathy, intuition, creativity, and strength. They became the roots that anchored me.

My self-awareness and self-esteem grew from there. I found value in who I was, not from outside validation but through my own eyes. No matter how much the wind of contradictions or challenge threatened me, I learned to stay upright.

I used to think that some people were just born happy, and the rest of us struggled to find joy. Now I no longer believed that. I now believed that there are those who are more connected to the things that make them happy, and those who are not as clear. Happiness is not an inherent state of mind, but rather it is born out of the things that we do and the thoughts that we think.

I started to pay attention to what was happening when I felt happy. When I was working, living my dream, staying on-purpose, shining my light, singing my song, dancing my dance, and completely fulfilling all the reasons for my presence here, I felt alive. I was immersed in present time, time went by super fast, and I felt really happy. When I was with my animals, Jay, and the kids, I felt happy. When my mind was racing with negative thoughts or I was not doing the things that create joy, I felt sad and anxious.

Whenever I was feeling unhappy, I learned to find something more fun to do or something else to focus on. The change in activity and thought brought a change in my mood almost instantly. Sometimes all it took to change my mood was to hug one of our cows.

Slowly I cultivated an idea of who I was and how to stay centered and happy.

Like Whisper though, to be truly happy I had to let go of

some things in my past that I'd been holding on to. I had to look at forgiveness. Each animal we had rescued had seen the worst of humanity and experienced unimaginable horrors. How did they forgive the human race? How did they come to trust and find joy again in our barnyards? Our animals understood the secret to forgiveness: forgiveness is never about the other person, to exonerate them or pardon their actions. Forgiveness is only about us, letting things go and setting ourselves free. If our animals could forgive, I certainly could too.

I was still carrying a lot of things from past relationships. There were people who came into my life and took something from me or hurt me in some way. I realized that it was time to let them go. Each day during my meditation, I would think of someone I was upset with, picture their face, and ask them for forgiveness. Once I asked sincerely for their forgiveness, I offered them mine. I would repeat this forgiveness exercise every day until I no longer carried any animosity toward that person. This allowed me to take my power back and take responsibility for what had happened, even if it wasn't my fault.

I repeated this until there were no longer any feelings when I thought of the person. I went down my list of people who had hurt me, one after the other, and eventually there was no one left that I felt angry with. I felt lighter and freer.

Some successful people I admire say that when they look back at their life, no matter what they have gone through, they don't regret a single thing. In fact, they claim they wouldn't change a thing. These are people who have been through war, famine, disease, loss, and tragedy, far beyond what most people experience. As much as I admired them, in the past I couldn't understand why they wouldn't have wanted to have suffered less. Now that I had accepted the totality of who I was, as I was, I got it. When I looked back at my life, I too didn't regret a single thing I'd been through. I realized it is the weakest moments of my life that have given me the greatest strength. The most painful things in my life have given me the greatest empathy for other people. The things I was the most ashamed of have given me the most resilience.

The animals at the Gentle Barn were the same way. The things that made them different were the very things that saved their lives. If Dudley was healthy, he would have been sent to slaughter with the others, but because he was missing a foot, we were able to save him. Our animals stood out and garnered attention because of their lameness, blindness, illness, or horrific circumstance. The animals showed us, again and again, that our challenges always turn out to be our superpower.

Instead of feeling ashamed at their differences, like we humans often do, I watched our animals get hurt and lost in order to find themselves. I saw them move through their suffering in order to help others. Even after so much of the world saw them as nothing but meat, without feelings or intelligence, they still continued to blossom into the healers and leaders that they truly were. I saw our animals demonstrate self-acceptance, gratitude, forgiveness, happiness, and resilience every day.

They taught me that when we have gone through trauma, suffered through an under-nurtured childhood, forgotten who we are or why we're here, we can, like our animals, take the darkest parts of our lives and turn them into the greatest gifts for ourselves and others.

Cows allow themselves to be, breathe, meditate, hold still, and connect to themselves and others in a deep way, without the self-judgment that we suffer as humans. They know that whether they're licking a newborn baby in support of a new mom, disciplining a teenager, leading a meditation session, or just chewing their cud, no experience is more important than another. They know that whether they're busy or relaxing, whether they're contributing or resting, they are worthy and valuable. Our animals taught me that when having a day off for self-care, I'm just as valuable as when I've put in an eighteen-hour workday. The rest is just as important as the work. Fun is just as important as effort.

Learning from the cows and other animals, I committed to taking my days off just as seriously as I do my workdays and setting aside time for myself the same way that I set aside time for my staff. I carved out time every morning to meditate and start my day with gratitude and positivity, just like the cows do at the Gentle Barn.

Our cows start eating at seven in the morning. After breakfast, they always groom each other, and then lie down to meditate. They make time to clear their minds, remember who they are, connect to themselves and each other, rid their minds of thought, and get open, vulnerable, and warm in preparation for our guests and the people who need them. Inspired by them, I also set my morning routine so that I could prepare myself for the day and give all my energy to everyone who needed me.

We cannot offer anyone a drink from an empty cup; we must fill our own cup first, then give the sustenance away to others.

Besides our wonderful cows, when I think of a perfect matriarch, I think of our pig Menorah. Like most cows, she too was used for breeding, being impregnated repeatedly and having her babies taken away. Once "worn out," she was sold to a family to eat for Christmas dinner. Mere days before that fateful Christmas, Menorah gave birth to a litter of piglets. Once the family saw her as a mom, they could no longer see her as a meal. They allowed us to drive from California to Washington state to bring Menorah and her babies home to the safety of the

Gentle Barn. Beyond Meat sponsored their rescue and donated a new trailer to drive them home in.

The drive there took a few days because we stopped at night to sleep. But with Menorah and the family in the trailer, we drove nonstop for the entire twenty-hour drive back from Washington. Thanks to taking turns driving, loud music, coffee, and Jay's persistence when I couldn't stay awake anymore, we made it home in one piece.

Instead of the pink pigs Jay and I were used to rescuing, Menorah was black with white underneath her face, neck, and belly. She had a long tail that curled around in a ringlet, a long snout, and intelligent dark-brown eyes. The piglets were orange with dark stripes running down the length of their bodies. They looked like orange watermelons and were about that same size. We did a holiday-themed naming auction, and with the help of participants from all over the world, Menorah's babies were named Dreidel, Mistletoe, Tinsel, Blitzen, Miracle, and Gingerbread.

We had rescued many pigs from slaughter, but only one at a time. This was the first time we rescued a family, and we were excited to watch Menorah parent and the babies grow. We created a nursery for them in the barn and made it private. We interacted with the family out in the yard but never intruded in their room unless we needed to fill water bowls and clean their hay beds. I remember back to when my children were born; privacy and the sanctity of undisturbed time with my babies was sacred. I wanted to provide Menorah with the same rights as any new mom.

Every day for months after their arrival, I'd sit in the barnyard, watching the piglets and looking for distinguishing marks that would help me differentiate them. Then, just when I was finally able to tell them apart, the piglets had their first growth spurt and transformed from striped babies to furry, brown pigs who looked more like bears, and I had to start the process all over again. They looked so much alike! But I finally figured it out.

There were four male piglets: Tinsel, the largest male, had reddish hair. Dreidel was the darkest piglet and in time grew from brown to almost black. He was the most like his mom. Blitzen had polka dots on his belly, and Miracle had a white tail. The two females were easier to tell apart, as Mistletoe kept her orange complexion and Gingerbread turned mousy brown.

When they first arrived, Menorah nursed her babies exactly every two hours. The piglets would be off exploring the yard and having fun, and like clockwork every two hours Menorah circled the yard, making a very distinct sound to call them. Once they were all rounded up, Menorah would roll onto her side and the babies would suckle. Menorah sang to them in sweet, soft grunts the whole time. Once their bellies were full, Menorah stood up and the piglets went back to playing and exploring, digging rivets in the ground with their snouts, splashing in the swimming pool, chewing on sticks, and chasing each other around like puppy dogs.

One day I was watching Menorah as she lay on her side, happily nursing her babies and singing to them when, all of a sudden, she jerked up in pain. She jumped up very quickly and whirled around to look at each baby until she found the culprit. Menorah growled at Gingerbread, angrily warning her to be more careful with her teeth. Gingerbread slinked off to the side of the pen, hanging her head for a while before being invited back to play with the others. She never bit her mom again.

When we introduced the piglets to food, at first mashed fruits and vegetables and then small chunks along with soaked grain, Menorah weaned the piglets to four times a day. When she was nursing them every two hours, she never went into the pool, even though it was warm out. When she started weaning them, she would go into the pool to distract them from nursing. I realized what her strategy was: while nursing frequently, she didn't go swimming because she didn't want her nipples to be dirty for her very young babies, but later she used the mud to help her wean them.

The more solid food the babies ate, the more Menorah weaned them, until months later they were only nursing before bedtime. At four months, when the piglets were big, active, and eating up a storm, Menorah decided that it was time to wean them completely. When she lay down, she tucked her legs in, offering her babies no access to milk. The babies tried hard to convince Menorah to roll over, but she held her ground until one by one they finally gave up and went to sleep in their fluffy hay beds. Once all the babies had fallen asleep, Menorah carefully tiptoed into bed next to them so she wouldn't wake them up. It took a few weeks, but by the time the babies were five months old, they were fully weaned.

When the babies were about a year old, Menorah decided she needed some space and time for herself in the evenings. Instead of going to bed with them, she put her kids to bed in one room and then, once they were all asleep, went to the next room to enjoy the evening with her grown-up friends.

Watching Menorah parent her babies was an affirmation that we are all the same, with the same needs for bonding with our babies, weaning them, disciplining them, and raising them to be kind, well behaved, happy, and healthy.

Menorah is smart, affectionate, and no-nonsense. Her babies understand that when she says *no*, it's no. She never rethinks her decisions or lets others change her mind. She knows when to walk away from a conflict because she does not come at things from ego. She knows when to hold her stance because she stands in her own certainty. She is sweet and affectionate but isn't afraid of using force when she must. She is fiercely protective of her family; she even chased goats and sheep out of her bedroom until the other animals learned to stay out. She rolls over for tummy rubs but does not do it to please us, and if she is not in the mood, she will walk away.

Watching Menorah parent her babies, I have accepted that being a matriarch is a difficult position. You have to be willing to be strongly disliked by those you love the most. As of this writing, all three of my children are now finished with high school and considered to be young adults. They want to decide their futures and push away from parental guidance, in the same way I did at their age. Although Jay and I both applaud their independence and respect their right to their own opinions, I will, like Menorah, step in if I feel that decisions are being made that have negative long-term consequences. This intervention is rarely invited or appreciated at the moment, but as I learned through Menorah, I am willing to live through the period of anger or rejection in order to protect my children's futures. If it took me into my fifties to really find myself, then I know that they too need their time of questioning and establishing their own authority. It's not easy for me to accept that I'm not the person they seek advice from, but I do let them know that I can't be pushed away. They are my kids, and I'm not going anywhere. That's what a matriarch does.

When her kids were fully grown, Menorah suddenly got ill and seemed to be in the end stages of kidney failure. We tried to load her onto the trailer to go to the hospital to get fluids, and she flat-out refused. Even after trying for two hours, Jay, our staff, and I could not change her mind. We had to find veterinarians who would come out to treat her at home and figure out other ways to support her. After trying to reason with her, and physically trying to lift her onto the trailer, I honored her wishes to remain at home with her babies.

Menorah was not being a scared, unintelligent animal who just didn't know better. She was a matriarch and knew what she was doing. Her refusal to go to the hospital was not arbitrary. She was probably wiser than us, with more foresight. She probably knew that the hospital would not be able to help her, and she didn't want to die there. She was respectfully letting us know that although she was seriously ill, she was not afraid and wanted to spend as much time as possible with her babies and the people who love her, in her sanctuary. After trying to convince her, I relented because I trusted her.

Menorah is a matriarch, and I look at her not just as an animal but as a goddess with a powerful voice. I would do anything to honor, obey, and adore her. Menorah knows who she is, knows how she feels, and knows what she wants. Like all matriarchs, Menorah has made peace with her past, is grateful for her life, and is full of love for all those around her.

At home, Menorah allowed me, my staff, and our veterinarians to give her intravenous and subcutaneous fluids and injections for pain relief, take her temperature, and put syringes of Pedialyte and nutritional supplements in her mouth. She held still for all exams. She wanted the help, she wanted more time, and she wanted to feel better; it's just that she was not willing to leave her home or her family. She had every right to make that decision for herself. I am sure that at the end of my life, I would probably make the same decision and would hope that my loved ones would respect it.

With all medical options failing, I was desperate for a way to help Menorah, so I started doing scaler wave energy healing on her twice a day. Each morning and evening before bed I sat in my meditation chair, closed my eyes, and went through Menorah's body in my mind, seeing her organs, bones, and chakras filled with healing light. I had seen it work on Karma years earlier and knew that it sure couldn't hurt.

After the first day Menorah seemed to be in less pain. The second day she started drinking on her own. The third day she ate oats and blueberries. The fourth day she ate huge bowls of fruit and vegetables throughout the day. When we did her last blood draw, Menorah's kidney values had drastically decreased. Menorah was on the mend, and she'd never had to leave home! I was learning about the undeniable power and value of energy healing and my place as the healer of our family.

The questions we have to ask ourselves are not about how big our waistline is, the color of our hair, how many wrinkles we have, or what our wardrobe looks like. Those are superficial things that leave us empty and scrambling once the answers are not to our liking. The better questions are things like, How do we treat waiters? Do we say *please* and *thank you*? Are we grateful? How do we respond to people or animals asking for help? Do we walk past them, treating them like they're invisible, or do we stop and do something? Are we as gentle as we can be? Do the things we eat and buy promote peace and kindness?

Little everyday decisions that we make every time we eat something, buy something, or go somewhere, add up. They have power behind them. They have consequences. They affect others. Every day I ask myself, How can I be kinder today? How can I be smarter today? How can I be more thoughtful today? When I lay my head down on the pillow at night, I set my intentions on being an even better instrument of peace the next day.

As I feel myself getting older, I want to make sure that the Gentle Barn is in good hands without me, that the animals will be safe, and our programs will continue. I have shifted my focus from creating and building the Gentle Barn to putting procedures into place, working with our board of directors, and training staff to continue my work long after I am gone. I want to make sure that the organization is always in good hands, no matter what.

Just like our matriarchs train the next leader to take care of things after they are gone, and I am setting up procedures for the Gentle Barn to run after Jay and I are gone, I think about our beautiful Mother Earth and how to set up future generations to care for her after we are all gone. As a species, we have evolved both physically and technologically. We shifted from matriarchal tribes with shamans and medicine women to men-run armies, governments, hospitals, and churches. Since then, this male energy has created many advances, but it has also polluted our oceans, cut down the forests, imprisoned our animals, filled our bodies with disease, and nearly destroyed our environment, all in the name of money. The pendulum has swung too far — we must bring back the feminine energy!

This is not about men versus women. This is about the masculine energy of domination, power, and money versus the feminine energy of creativity, intuition, empathy, community, family, healing, protection, and love. We must redefine female and male roles in our society. We must raise our boys to connect with their feelings; be intuitive, empathetic, and open; and cry when they need to. We must teach them to respect women and be unafraid of female power.

We have to raise our daughters to speak up for themselves; be strong, courageous, fierce, and brave; have opinions; and stand up for what is right. We must show our girls how to respect and accept their bodies, to feel beautiful, and to eventually be the matriarchs the world needs.

CHAPTER FOURTEEN

MAGIC

Simple pleasures might seem pleasing at first,
but being of service is always the deepest delight.

— MAGIC

America was built on the backs of horses and donkeys. When the first Europeans came to the East Coast, horses helped them build roads, bridges, and houses. When they started expanding from the East Coast to the West Coast, they traveled in horse-drawn covered wagons or on horseback. The California gold rush happened on the backs of horses and donkeys, and the railroad system across the country was built with the help of horses pulling huge tree trunks and steel rails. When Henry Ford revolutionized motorized vehicles, little by little we stopped our dependence on horses for transportation; and with the Industrial Revolution, for labor. Of course, horse lovers still kept horses for their own enjoyment.

On August 10, 2022, a Central Park carriage horse named Ryder collapsed in the middle of the street in Manhattan. It was one of the city's hottest months in recorded history. Ryder was already old and underweight, with visible ribs on both sides. The driver should have immediately untethered him from the carriage and given him a chance to recover. A huge and horrified crowd surrounded the fallen horse, watching as the driver flogged him, yelling "Get up! Get up!" Videos shot with shocked onlookers' cellphones went viral. The police arrived, pulling the driver away and using a hose to cool down the heat-exhausted horse. It took Ryder four hours to stand up, and then he was loaded onto a trailer and driven away.

In New York City, horse-drawn carriages are a time-honored tradition, despite poor working conditions for the horses. Featured in many films as an image of romance or family fun, the gorgeous steeds pull carriages around Central Park year-round, in the heat and humidity of summer and the blizzards of the New Year. The clickety-clack of their hooves on cement or asphalt and the Cinderella coachman attire of the driver have appealed to tourists since the park first opened in 1858. In reality, however, there is very little magic for the horses doing all the work, day in and day out.

The horses are surrounded on either side by cars, honking horns, and pollution. They inhale the fumes of passing trucks and buses while they stand on concrete, waiting for the next load of people to pull through the park. Then, late at night, the carriage is driven back to a concrete building, where the horse is sheltered until early the next morning, when their day begins all over again. New York City carriage horses do not get to frolic in green pastures or socialize with other horses, even though they are extremely social animals. When the horses are too injured or old to pull, they get sold at auction to slaughterhouses, an ungrateful thanks for years of obedience and hard work.

After seeing the videos of Ryder, Jay immediately flew to New York in the hopes of bringing him home to the Gentle Barn for a much-deserved retirement. Jay did get an audience with the spokesperson of the carriage horse association, who made promises, then disappeared, and months later reported that Ryder had been euthanized.

Fortunately, Jay was able to rescue two other carriage horses who had worked themselves to "uselessness" and were being sent to the slaughterhouse. For now, they live at the Gentle Barn Missouri, but our dream is to acquire property in upstate New York for a Gentle Barn that could be home to carriage horses and many other animals.

Shortly after Jay and I married, I decided that my days of horseback riding were over. As much as I had loved it as a child and through my twenties and thirties, I felt better and enjoyed my time more when I was walking beside the horse. Because so many of our horses were previously in situations of hardship or abuse, we promise them that they will never have to feel the bind of a saddle or carry humans on their backs, for pleasure or for work.

Every rescued horse at the Gentle Barn has relished their newfound freedom, and their joy-filled prances through the pasture assure me that it's the right thing to do for them. Except for one horse, named Magic.

Magic came to us when he was only a few months old. He had belonged to an animal trainer for the movies. Because Magic was a paint horse, exquisitely colored with swirly white, brown, and black patterns, the trainer thought he would be perfect for the movie industry. Magic loved the lessons, enjoyed learning, and thrived with the sense of accomplishment. Tragically, several months later, the man and his wife got divorced, and in the divorce, they decided to sell not only all their property, but all their animals as well. They heard about the Gentle Barn and brought Magic to us.

We settled Magic into our barn, acclimating him to our routines and introducing him to our other horses. Instead of thriving, though, Magic fell into a deep depression. He stood listlessly, with his neck down and his head resting on the ground. He didn't want to eat. He didn't want to interact with us. I started worrying that he might not make it. I parked myself in his stall and talked to him, explaining what his life would look like with us, and little by little he started bonding and connecting with me.

Once we had breathed life back into him, Magic started enjoying his days at the Gentle Barn. The other horses took a liking to him and, knowing he was a youngster, were kind to him, even taking turns standing watch over him as he slept. He finally started to grow, and his personality blossomed.

We thought Magic's life was perfect, a life that any horse would envy. All our other horses had been beaten down before coming to us, but Magic got to grow up in the safety of the Gentle Barn, never facing any adversity. He would never have to wear a saddle or be ridden. Someone would hand-walk him every day, or he'd go on adventures with us. There were a dozen other horses to play with, and he would always have his needs met.

But by the time Magic was five years old, he was miserable. Every time he would see me, he would run to the rails, put his mouth on the metal bars, and inhale air into his gut. Called *cribbing*, this usually is what horses do to self-soothe when they spend most of their time in tiny stalls and are robbed of interaction. I never in my wildest dreams expected one of the Gentle Barn horses to crib.

I asked Magic, "Why are you so miserable?"

"You've ruined my life," he told me.

"You have a great life. How is it bad?"

He answered, "Do you see me? Look at me. Look how gorgeous I am. I'm obviously born to perform. I was born to be the center of attention, to learn tricks and to leap in the air and to twirl and to please people. I want to hear applause and prance in a spotlight. But instead, I'm in a dusty pasture with old horses, and my life is rotting away."

"Magic, what do you want me to do?"

"I want you to send me somewhere where I can perform and fulfill my destiny."

I just could not believe the irony! Millions of horses who

are forced to pull, run, carry humans, and work would give anything to be at the Gentle Barn to rest, and here was Magic, who can spend his whole life in luxury, and he wanted to work!

Trying to honor this show business horse and give him what he wanted, I called a handful of animal trainers to ask if they wanted to work with Magic. They all said that they had their own animals. I even called Cirque du Soleil to ask if they wanted to work with him, but they said they breed their own horses. To appease Magic, I found a horse trainer to come to the house each week and play with him. He could learn tricks, or explore the trails, or play games to stimulate his mind. We also placed Magic as the focal point in every tour and open Sunday. With a built-in audience, Magic could perform and receive applause if he wanted to.

This was better than nothing, but it was still not enough for Magic. He kept complaining, telling me I'd ruined his life. Magic started threatening that if I did not fix things, he was going to end up getting sick. I was turning myself into a pretzel trying to help and didn't know what else to do.

Sure enough, a few months later, Magic was hospitalized.

When I visited him, he said, "See? I told you. You've got to make this right."

I replied, "I'll try harder. I'll try more people. I'll make more calls. Please just come home."

Magic recovered and came home, and I tried harder and made more calls. But I got nowhere. No reputable trainer had room for him, and I was not going to hand him off to a stranger, no matter how much he begged. Barely recovered from the last hospitalization, Magic started up with the threats: that if I didn't send him somewhere exciting, he would colic again.

A year later, Magic landed back at the hospital.

Again, I visited him and pleaded, "Magic, please. I love

you. I want you, I need you. Please come home. I will keep trying to make you happy."

He got better and came home, still insisting that he needed
more.

Jay and I brought Magic to our Sun Chlorella Healing Center, in the hopes that the change of scenery would be stimulat-
ing and make him happy. It worked for a while. He perked up,
met new horses, walked on new trails, and played new games
with his trainer each week. But a few months later when the
novelty wore off and the new routine turned stale, he was back
to cribbing, threatening, and complaining.

When Magic ended up in the hospital for the third time, I
snapped. I couldn't take the guilt anymore; I couldn't take the
pressure. I told Magic I had done all I could. I'd made a million
calls, hired a trainer, brought an audience to him, and given
him a life that any horse on this planet would beg for. I told
Magic that if all I had done was not enough, if he was truly miserable, if he wanted to die that badly, then maybe he should go!

That shut him up! I called his bluff, and Magic has not
threatened me or been hospitalized since.

Magic was still vain and got away with rude behavior with
the females because of his good looks. But he made friends and
started making peace with his life. He started enjoying his sessions with his trainer even more; they came up with a whole
repertoire of tricks and then taught us the cues. He nodded Yes,
shook his head No, counted by pawing his foot on the ground,
gave hugs with his neck, gave kisses with his mouth, and even
bowed. Our guests were delighted, and so was Magic.

When the herd's matriarch and later the lead male passed
away of old age, I noticed a shift in Magic. He had matured,
become gracious and generous. Instead of competing for female attention, he nuzzled the others, both males and females.
Instead of barging through the gate first for dinner, he allowed

others to go first. He started mitigating arguments instead of causing them. Our little movie star was becoming the lead male of our horse herd! He had matured into being a patriarch and began taking the role very seriously.

Stepping into his new role, Magic seemed happier than he had ever been before. He had new purpose and seemed to step higher and hold his head with new pride. He no longer complained about his life and was much more focused on his family than on performing. Instead of asking to go somewhere fun, he didn't want to leave. Taking care of his family became everything. Doing tricks and making people laugh or applaud seemed silly once he realized that giving to others was the true magic of life.

During the pandemic, we heard from a family who could no longer afford to keep their horse, Bonnie, because they had fallen on hard times. Having never been in an abusive situation, Bonnie arrived at the Gentle Barn with a lot of courage and confidence. Since we had not had a matriarch in our horse pasture for years, we were hopeful that Bonnie might eventually take that role.

It took Bonnie barely any time at all. She went happily into the horse family, like the long-awaited mother who would give stability and direction to all. To this day, she stands her ground in a loving way and has restored peace and balance within the family. Bonnie has enthusiastically accepted her new role as a leader and matriarch, and we are all grateful.

There is an old Chinese curse that says, "May you get what you want." The curse implies that we may want a great many things, but sometimes we find out that we are better off getting something else instead. The Universe, Creator, Spirit knows what is ultimately best for us, and to get everything we want would be a curse, not a blessing.

In my late teen years and early twenties, I really wanted to be an actress. I wanted to take on new and exciting roles and see myself on the big screen. Looking back now, I thank my lucky stars that acting didn't work out for me and I was able to found the Gentle Barn instead. Just like Magic, I thought the glamour and the attention would bring meaning into my life. But the truth is that for me and Magic, serving, caring, supporting, and giving to others offers a much greater high than applause or accolades, any day!

Magic still turns it on for our Gentle Barn visitors, but after a while, he lets the curtain drop as he returns to guiding, guarding, and giving his attention and affection to his own extended family.

CHAPTER FIFTEEN

SURRENDER

Sometimes life is so overwhelming that the only option is
to get out of the way and surrender.

— DELILAH

I had heard that a tornado sounds like a freight train plowing by, inches from your ears. On a spring night at the Gentle Barn Tennessee, that exact noise had me cowering on the laundry room floor, holding Sky in my arms and pleading with God.

Jay and I had spent a ten-hour day training staff and visiting animals. We were exhausted and ready to collapse into bed when we got alerts on our phones, ordering us to take shelter immediately. A tornado had been spotted in the area. Not having a basement or knowing exactly what to do, I called Sky and ran downstairs. Jay headed to the door to make sure the animals were secure, commanding me over his shoulder to stay inside.

At first, I wasn't concerned. Perhaps it was an alert for the entire state of Tennessee and not necessarily local to us. Then I started wondering. Was it for Nashville, and so would be farther away? Or was it for our immediate area, and we were in more danger than we thought?

Then I heard the deafening noise: creepy, eerie, evil even. It shook me to my core. I grabbed Sky and we both lay on the floor of our laundry room, the only room without windows. It is amazing how religious I become when I am in a crisis. With nothing else to do, I kept repeating over and over, "Please God help me, please God help me, please God protect Jay and our animals, please God help us!!"

As I lay there on the floor, my heartbeat racing and close to hyperventilating, I thought about how much I still wanted to accomplish. I had so many more dreams. I wanted to see my kids get older and to know my grandkids. "Please God help me, please God help me, please God help me!"

Jay, hearing the noise roar over the velocity of the wind, turned toward the house. Everything was pitch-black except when the lightning struck. With each illumination, like an old black-and-white film projected on a screen, he saw the trees bent sideways and could tell the tornado was headed for the house. He watched, horror-struck, thinking he was watching me die. Then, at the last minute, Jay saw the tornado lift up over the roof and disappear.

The whole time I lay on the floor with my arm around my dog chanting, "Please God help me, please God help me, please God help me!" I had no choice but to surrender to whatever would happen. There was no place to run, no way to change the course of nature.

There is a time for action, forward movement, problem-solving, making plans, creating dreams, and then there is a time for surrender. It is in times of natural disaster that we most know we are not solely in charge, that there are forces greater than ours. We had evacuated from two fires, lived through a huge earthquake, and survived a tornado headed for our house. These experiences taught me that in the face of great natural power, we are small and defenseless, and sometimes we must surrender to our fate, to our destinies, to our Maker. That night I was given another chance to create, dream, grow, love and be loved, heal and be healed, and I was grateful. The miracle of life in the face of that tornado pushed me even further into self-care, gratitude, finding joy in every moment, and living every day to the fullest, not taking a minute for granted.

With the help of our cows and other animals, I had finally learned who I was, accepted myself as I am, figured out what I needed to do to make myself happy, set boundaries to protect myself, learned how to combat compassion fatigue, established how to walk someone home with grace, forgiven the past, and realized that when animals transition, they do not leave us.

Yet there was one more way in which I would finally learn to surrender. Not being able to save and rescue every hurting animal had always made me feel helpless. The only way to protect myself from that pain was to guard myself against hearing about or seeing animals I could not save. It wasn't denial; I just had to protect my heart and my nervous system from a constant state of stress.

Jay and I spent countless hours traveling by plane and then more hours by car, commuting from one Gentle Barn location to another. On the open stretches of highway, we often saw transport trucks full of cows headed to slaughter. On one trip, we were driving parallel to a transport trailer. The traffic was thick, and for over ten minutes we had to inch along beside this trailer with about eighty doomed cows in it.

At first I tried to look away, but my gaze was irresistibly drawn into the eyes of a gorgeous Holstein with beautiful black and white markings. I closed my eyes, already stinging with tears, and asked for permission to speak to her. I offered her my condolences for the way she and her family were being treated and the state of our cruel world. I explained that I and many others were working hard to share their story, be their voice, and create a gentler world.

Her reply was jaw-dropping. She told me not to feel sorry or sad. She said that she and her family were not afraid because they would soon be going home and that would be good.

How in the world could they be that brave, knowing they were going to die?

Baffled by her response, I needed an explanation. In the quiet stillness of my mind, breathing slowly with my eyes closed, I searched for answers. Did her acquiescence mean it was OK for those cows to go to their deaths? Was she insinuating that eating animals was now somehow OK? I had dedicated my entire life to rescuing animals from slaughter, and now suddenly this cow tells me not to worry?!

The message I got back was simple: It is always and forever blissful once we leave our bodies. We do not need to cry for the departed. The work we are doing is not for those transitioning, but for the people capable of violence. The darkness in our world today is there with the men and women working at slaughter-houses, killing animals; working in dairies, taking babies away from their moms; and working at poultry farms, imprisoning birds just for their eggs. The darkness is in people who are blind to animals' light, innocence, and beauty. Apathy and a lack of love are the true tragedy on our planet that needs to be healed.

I thought about how often I cringed and looked away when passing the remains of a wild animal who had been killed trying to cross a highway or busy road. I would squeeze my eyes shut, not wanting to see evidence of an awful death. But now I was being offered a very different way to think of their passing, a way I could never have come up with on my own.

The idea I received that day helped me think about death in a different way. For an animal struck and killed by a car, for example — on the physical plane there is a body, mangled and bloody, tragically killed on the road. However, from the animal's point of view, stepping out of their body and expanding to spirit feels the same whether the animal was hit by a car or passed gently in their sleep; it is always wonderful to go home. Whether we pass away when we are young, are killed violently, or transition at the end of a good, long life, surrounded by friends and family, transitioning always feels wonderful, peaceful, and loving. By cringing at the sight of a deceased animal, I was experiencing my own perspective of their transition and missing theirs.

Now when Jay and I drive by a dead animal, I whisper, "Welcome home," acknowledging the animal's perspective and allowing the miracle of the transition no matter what the circumstances. It helps me honor the truth of the animal's homecoming instead of seeing the disfigured remains as the only truth. It makes me feel a lot better as well.

I thought about another outcome that I had to surrender to, which happened a few years before the tornado. There was a news article about two teenage girls in Oregon raising a young cow named Red Box. In the article photo, Red Box looked like my Buddha and Dudley. He had fuzzy red fur, a white face, white socks, beautiful, long, white eyelashes, and fluffy red ears. The article described how these girls bottle-fed him when he was a baby, halter-trained him, played with him, and taught him to come running when they called out his name. He was like a puppy dog who played fetch and laid down for snuggles. They loved this cow.

Unfortunately, they were raising him for Future Farmers of America, a national organization that encourages schoolkids to pursue careers in animal agriculture. The kids get to raise baby animals, and upon graduation, they send their animals to slaughter. The kids earn money and other recognitions for their so-called achievements. The article said that Red Box had become the girls' best friend and that they were really sad they had to slaughter him. To justify it, they decided to use his meat to feed the homeless.

Red Box's face was absolutely beautiful and innocent, and I couldn't stop thinking about him or the young women who raised him. I shared the article with Jay in the hopes that we could come up with a way to resolve this situation. Over the next few months, we considered the options: Maybe we could open a Gentle Barn in Oregon, where Red Box could live and the girls could volunteer. What if Red Box would give healing to people who needed him, and we could feed vegan food to the homeless, not once, but every year of Red Box's life? We even came up with a donor who agreed to give $20,000 to the girls' school and further their education in plant-based agriculture. This idea was good for the cow, the students, the school, and the community.

Unable to get through on the phone, Jay boarded a plane to Oregon to pitch our idea to the school principal in person. The principal was very receptive to Jay but said we needed the students to agree. He said he would present the idea to the class the next day, and the class would vote on it.

The next morning, while the students deliberated and cast their votes, Jay was waiting impatiently in his hotel room and I was pacing back and forth at the Gentle Barn California. Finally, the phone rang, and I answered immediately. I was completely shocked when Jay told me the class had voted to go through with the slaughter.

I had not seen that coming. Why would they kill somebody if we're offering such a wonderful way to keep them alive? I slumped down to my knees, my shoulders hunched over in defeat, tears rolling down my face. How would a group of children vote to kill an animal they loved? It made no sense.

I closed my eyes, breathed in and out a few times, centered myself, cleared my brain of thoughts, and asked for a different perspective, a different way to look at the situation. In the stillness, I realized that the kids in that classroom were born and raised in their farming community. They had probably seen animals slaughtered since the time they were toddlers and thought of it as part of life. In that context, how could they possibly have made any other choice? Those kids were raised and groomed to cast that vote.

On the other hand, what if those schoolchildren had access to a sanctuary where they could see animals' intelligence, affection, and personality? What if they had been exposed to other human beings who worked to save animals? That is why sanctuaries are so important — they give people the perspective needed to make gentler choices.

That answer inspired me to bring more people to the Gentle Barn and to help others open sanctuaries in their states. Jay and I even came up with a twelve-week course to teach people how to start their own sanctuaries, which we now teach to people all over the country.

I think people are basically born good, connected to animals and to their own feelings. Apathy, disconnection, racism, and hatred are not inherent, but taught. We can combat those lessons by exposing as many people as possible to a gentler option, where we protect instead of destroy, stand up for justice instead of turn a blind eye, and use our resources not for our own good but for the good of everyone. This drive to save, heal, share, and create good in our communities and in our children is also part of who I am. It is good.

At the end of each day, there is still so much more work that needs to be done. No matter how many animals we rescue, there are still millions more who need help. No matter how many go vegan, there are still too many people eating animals and supporting their suffering. We can work as hard as we can, do as much as we can, but at some point, to prevent ourselves from going insane, the only thing left to do is surrender.

In life, there are many things that don't make any sense, and I just have to surrender to the truth that I don't have the answer and may never have the answer. For example, we have two very old roosters in our Nashville location; Rick Springfield has heart disease and Rosey has cancer. In Gentle

Barn California, we have a perfectly happy and lively three-year-old rooster, Meep. It is Rick and Rosey who are thriving, while Meep passed away unexpectedly in his sleep, leaving us all baffled. Why? Why did Victory and David pass away at a very young age, while our chicken Tulip is way past her expected life span at fourteen and still going strong? Why have we been able to save so many in such rough shape, yet sometimes an animal in the same condition doesn't make it, no matter what we do or how hard we try?

The key to life on this planet is to remember who we are and why we have come, as quickly as possible. Once we know those two things, we must figure out what we want to do and why. In this, it's best to leave the "how" to the Universe. It's best to follow the ideas, inspiration, and impulses we get, and then surrender the rest. Some things we can create, and other things we must let go of and see what happens.

One Saturday morning in California, we heard sirens down the street and wondered what was going on. Seconds later we heard a knock on the door. The neighbors excitedly told us that a bull was running down the middle of Sierra Highway and several attempts to catch him had failed. They wondered if we could help. We immediately pulled our boots on, yelled for our staff, jumped in the car, and headed to where the bull was last seen.

When we got there, we saw not a bull but a frightened female cow, running wide-eyed and terrified round and round while animal control staff and the neighbors tried to catch her with swinging ropes. We asked them to stop for a minute, to give her time to catch her breath. Then while I talked reassuringly to her, one of our animal caretakers walked slowly up to her and took ahold of her horns. She rested in his grasp until

Jay pulled the trailer around, opened its back door, and escorted her inside.

One of the animal control people asked if we might be willing to keep her at our house until they could find out who she belonged to. We agreed, and luckily, no one ever claimed her. After a few weeks we were able to officially adopt her, naming her Delilah. I don't know if she was injured and then escaped, or was injured while she escaped, but once she was off the trailer, safe inside our pasture, and her adrenaline had worn off, we noticed she had an injured pelvis with a very pronounced limp.

Not only was she lame, but she had an intense hatred for humans. If any of us walked near her enclosure, she would charge and violently smash her horns into the steel fencing. It was a challenge to feed her without being impaled. We wanted to show her that humans could be kind and that she was safe with us. The challenge was, how would we be able to treat her injuries without losing a chance at the trust we hoped to have with her? Or should we build trust and forgo the pelvis? Either choice came with a downside that would affect the rest of her life.

I decided to surrender and let it go for a few days to see if the answers found me. Two days later we got a busload of energy healers who came to the Gentle Barn to practice what they had learned after a weeklong course. Our animals were only too happy to oblige, enjoying the company, attention, and the good energy healing that the group brought. After I greeted them, described the Gentle Barn, and explained what we did, the healers dispersed and found animals to work on. One or more students stood in front of an animal, held up their hands, and exuded energy to their eager recipients.

A crowd of healers were drawn to Delilah and encircled her. Instead of charging them angrily like she had with us, Delilah stood calmly in the center of their circle. The men and women held their hands up and emitted energy to her for over an hour. When they left and boarded their bus, the animals all seemed happy, the students were thrilled to have gained experience, and the property felt sparkly and uplifting. It was a good evening, but I didn't give it much more thought at the time.

The next morning, I went down to check on the animals and greet them, handing out cookies as I went. When I arrived at Delilah's enclosure, instead of charging me as she usually did, she walked slowly over to me without a limp. I thought I was seeing things, so with cookies I lured her to walk around the entire pasture. The very severe limp and drag of her hind leg had vanished, never to return. Delilah was completely sound!

Sometimes when we want something badly but aren't getting it right away, or when we have a difficult choice to make but can't decide what to do, it's OK to surrender, let it go, leave it for a few days, and let the Universe help out. If I had brought in a veterinarian to see Delilah, she would have seen me as one of the many humans who had betrayed her and done her wrong. Had I left her injury alone to gain her trust, I would have been neglecting a physical ailment, and I would not have been able to live with that.

I needed a way to heal her and gain her trust at the same time, but I had no idea how to do that. I surrendered, and two days later, the Universe brought me a busload of energy healers, who repaired her pelvis without laying a hand on her. This restored her body and helped her trust us, just in time for Delilah to give birth to the son we hadn't known was growing in her belly.

When Delilah unexpectedly gave birth to her son, whom we named Charlie, they were both outside with all the other cows. Because we had never betrayed her trust, Delilah allowed us to carry her son to the nursery, where we had created a space for mom and baby to spend some time bonding,

stay dry and warm, and be safe from predators until Charlie
was a bit older.

Whenever I have surrendered, the Universe has never let
me down.

For the past twenty-three years, being the founder of the Gentle Barn has meant sacrificing time with my loved ones, not
taking many lunch breaks or vacations, neglecting myself, and
giving everything I had over to everyone else. I approached
the work of rescuing animals and having a sanctuary with the
mindset of a martyr.

Learning from the cows, I'm starting to realize that there is
activism in rest, and activism in self-care. I am now reinventing
my idea of a sanctuary. Instead of feeling broke, like I need to
sacrifice everything, I am going to feel wealthy with purpose.
I can give to others and give to myself at the same time. I can
create a work-life balance, where I'm giving the Gentle Barn my
all and also taking my days off.

I think many of us who are obsessed with animals come
from a very wounded place. We start out as victims and have
painful, lonely, sad pasts. There's often something broken inside of us that drives us to want to save the most innocent.

But the cows at the Gentle Barn become cow hug therapists only when they have healed; they cannot do it while they
are still broken. Seeing this led me to wonder: How can I help
animals overcome their victimization if I myself am coming
from a victim mentality? Before I can truly help animals from
being victims, I had to heal the damage inside of me.

Inspired by our cows, I have resolved to stop seeing myself
as damaged or defective in any way and, instead, have pledged
to see myself as whole. We need to be healed in order to heal

others. We have to love ourselves to be able to love anyone else. We have to fix that victim mentality inside of us before we can create a world where animals are free.

We are all spiritual beings, and we're all connected. We are all the same, no matter what species, gender, age, nationality, or religion we are. Underneath all the different labels is the same spirit, soul, and life force. We are all deeply connected to every rock, drop of water, leaf, sun, moon, star, and living creature, because we are all made of the same goods.

I look at incarnating into physical form as similar to when an FBI agent goes undercover. There's a place the FBI agent comes from, and there's a place he is going to once his assignment is over. When he is on assignment, however, the details of his undercover story, like his name, relationships, and job, might become very real to him. He might even get addicted to drugs or fall in love with the very perpetrator he is trying to bust. He might get lost and forget who he really is, believing his undercover identity more than his real one.

I believe that we all come from Spirit; that is who we really are. When we come here, it is like getting an undercover identity: we receive our gender, name, religion, race, family of origin, likes, dislikes, and individual set of circumstances. Some of us remember that we are really Spirit and are just "undercover" here, but all too many of us forget where we have come from and who we really are and start believing the undercover story a bit too much. Just like an FBI agent has daily phone calls with his handlers to remind him of who he really is and where he really came from, we can use meditation much the same way, to connect back to the truth of who we are.

Meditation has become my lifeline. When I first started to learn meditation, it seemed unbearable. I couldn't sit still or stop my mind from racing constantly. But meditation is like any other muscle, and with practice and repetition come advancements. Like Cow Hug Therapy, meditation has also become a thing I can return to whenever I need to remember who I am. I close my eyes and just breathe, letting my thoughts quiet and eventually go still, until I can connect with Spirit again. When I can pause my "trying to figure it out" and surrender to only being still, I can feel peace and calm, and there I can find answers and ideas that my harried brain might never let me hear. And when I open my eyes to greet the rest of the day, maybe I don't have to take everything so seriously.

Maybe we have challenges going on in our lives, but we can still remember that none of those things are our truth. As all our cows have taught me, a physical ailment isn't the truth of me. I am larger than life, no matter what my body is doing. The truth of me is my tremendous life force, which was here before I was born and is something I will still have when I'm done with my body.

I used to make excuses, like, "Oh, I don't have time to meditate." But now there is not one single day without meditation. I will always make time for it. I might have a shorter meditation on busier days, but every day I sit in my chair, close my eyes, and remember who I am, what I'm capable of, and why I'm here. The best type of surrender is to give your true self the love and time to be heard and honored.

CHAPTER SIXTEEN

GRATITUDE

There is love all around us. When we lose love,
we can always find a new adventure, a new story,
a new romance, when we stay open.

— HERO

Our current culture, including social media, can easily make a person feel like it's impossible to keep up or measure up. Add in all the negative news and the barrage of headlines designed to grab our attention — tearing people down, describing crime, disease, fraud, deceit, and violence, and sowing fear — it can feel like an uphill battle to feel positive. In a society that is now molded to always look for what's "wrong," it's easy to find reasons to complain. It's become so expected, and even accepted, that we may not even realize how often we complain at work, at home, and in our communities and the larger world.

One of the most significant lessons I've learned in rescuing, caring for, and communicating with animals is about gratitude. Gratitude is the antidote to the negative complaint virus that can take over our day-to-day lives.

Over the course of my life and work, I've had the good fortune to watch as thousands of animals let go of past neglect and even atrocities, which most humans would find it hard to get over, and welcome a better experience. They don't drag the past into the present but move forward with gratitude, accepting the care and the gifts of healing offered.

At some point I decided to begin living in a mindset of gratitude, like the animals at the Gentle Barn. Every day, I count my blessings for all that I have. My day-to-day problems could very easily become complaints if I allowed them to. With three locations, two hundred animals, over sixty staff members, almost a thousand volunteers, dozens of barns, innumerable fences and pieces of equipment, loads of schedules and calendars to maintain, there are always a handful of issues every week. In the same way our animals find and express gratitude, I now look at the big picture and the hundreds, if not thousands, of ways that things are going well.

One of our best examples of how gratitude increases the potential for more happiness is our horse Hero at the Gentle Barn California. Hero is an Appaloosa mare who in her younger years was gray with brown spots along her rump. She is now completely white. She was rescued from severe abuse and neglect and delivered to the Gentle Barn by animal control. When she shakily stepped off the trailer, Jay and I were both stunned by her terrible physical condition. She was emaciated from not having enough nutrition, and she was covered in caked-on mud and her own feces from lying down in a wet and filthy pen. On her knee, we could see some exposed bone at the base of an infected wound. She had obviously not been provided with shelter or shade from the California sun, as she was suffering from cancer in both eyes. The heinous conditions she had survived were enough to turn anyone into a shut-down, angry, violent, human-hating monster. But not Hero. As soon as she stepped from the trailer to the stall, she looked me in the eyes and asked for help.

Jay and I carefully bathed her, uncovering the fact that she wasn't a dark brown horse at all, she was just filthy. As we washed her down a second time, her light-colored fur coming through, she didn't flinch away from the sudsy water. In fact, she seemed to relish the chance to have someone touch her and care for her from head to toe. After the vet checked her and treated her wound, she began eating the fresh hay on offer with a smile on her face. And the bedtime cookies delighted her!

A couple days after her arrival, I was treating and rebandaging her knee in the middle of a storm. The rainfall was so hard I couldn't hear anything but the pelting water drumming on the roof of the stall. Every two minutes or so the sky would thunder, with lightning shooting across the horizon. I was jumpy and nervous, but Hero held perfectly still, carefully planting her feet so she would not step on me.

After a few months, the veterinarian determined that her right eye was beyond saving and had to be removed. Her left eye was not in good condition either, and her eyesight would always be extremely limited. After she recovered from the surgery, we knew we couldn't send her out into the pasture safely, yet we wanted her to have the companionship of other horses. Hero started spending time with our gelding Cherokee, and he soon became her seeing-eye horse. He would lead her to the water, to shade from the sun, and back home to the stable for dinner.

Hero fell in love with Cherokee. They were always together and did everything in tandem. My fondest memory is of the two of them side by side under a shade tree, lazily swishing their tails, eyes closed in private conversation.

When Cherokee passed away, despite her grief, Hero accepted another horse, Patric, who stepped in to help guide her through her day. After Patric, it was Rascalina, and afterward it was Lance, and then Bonsai.

One by one, Hero has loved and outlived seven horses who became her companions for a span of time. Instead of feeling unrelenting sorrow and defeat at losing the companions she loved so much, Hero always puts her heart on the line again. She takes the risk to love deeply.

During the pandemic, we rescued a beautiful white miniature horse named Marvel. He was found at an auction in Oklahoma that was preparing to send a hundred and seventy miniature horses to slaughter, including Marvel. Luckily, they were saved and brought to a rescue in Southern California, and we adopted Marvel when he was the last one left who needed a home. Hero was smitten with her diminutive new friend, who now takes her everywhere with him. Marvel is Hero's eighth partner!

Because of her hard past, Hero today walks with a limp, her knee is disfigured with scar tissue, and she is mostly blind. But if you experienced only her joy-filled presence, you would never know she had faced such hardships. She goes through her days grateful for every little snack of hay, sip of fresh water, and bedtime cookie. Hero is sweet to everyone, content wherever she is and with whoever wants to be with her. Hero leans into her massage therapy, stands still for acupuncture, comes running for energy healing, and appreciates everything that we do for her. Her capacity to open her heart again, to live without fear, and to accept the gifts and miracles of companionship is something I try to emulate in my life. She's my hero.

Another gratitude hero is Lolli, a little goat who lives at Gentle Barn Tennessee. She was born in the dead of winter, and because her previous owners offered her no shelter or warmth, she lost her back limbs to frostbite. She dragged herself around her yard for the first eight months of her life, trying to keep up with the other goats there. A concerned neighbor grew tired of watching Lolli suffer and reached out to us for help. We were able to remove Lolli and her mom, Minnie Mae, from that situation and welcome them home to the Gentle Barn. Lolli had surgery to remove a bone spur and was fit with prosthetic legs. Once she was full grown, she received a little supportive wheelchair that holds up her body so she can move around on her own.

Lolli can't jump up on surfaces or leap in the air like our other goats, and yet she has never complained. She is grateful for each morsel of hay, each piece of the wood shavings that make up her soft bed, and the stroke of each gentle hand. Lolli does not concentrate on the things she can't do but is ecstatic about the things she can do. When Gentle Barn guests meet her for the first time, they might think, "Oh, poor little girl. She must have gone through so much." While they are having that thought, Lolli is busy racing around the yard, headbutting playfully with her mom, and thinking, "Did you see how fast my wheelchair can go?!"

We rescued two donkeys in Missouri named Chance and Remi. They had been grossly neglected and came home with overgrown hooves, matted fur, and a fear of humans. It did take a while for them to learn to trust us, but now that they have opened their hearts to us, they spend every day in bliss and their past neglect is the furthest thing from their minds. They have forgiven the past and are grateful for each and every day. They chase each other around, wrestle like puppies, and hee-haw for more cookies. They explore the yard, come when we call them, and hold still for daily grooming.

I can tell you the story of each one of our two hundred animals across our three locations and come up with this same lesson from each of them: animals practice gratitude instead of complaint and have much to teach us about the subject!

As I've made my way through my own journey of self-discovery and growth and watched thousands of animals recover at the Gentle Barn, I have noticed that animals tend to heal faster and easier than most people. When animals are in abusive and neglectful circumstances, they suffer. When they are removed from those circumstances and come to trust their new family, they blossom. In contrast, when we humans are in abusive and neglectful circumstances, we also suffer, and in addition, we make beliefs about ourselves and the world that we take with us. Once we are removed from that negative experience and in a place where we are safe, loved, and cared for, the beliefs that we bring with us often continue to get in the way of our happiness.

We can learn from our wounds, but when we carry them with us into our present and our future, then we only continue to suffer the injury again and again. In the same way, exposing our daily lives to negative news and social media that blames, names, and shames will never create our happiness or gratitude, today or ever. It's time to stop and ask why we would choose to treat ourselves so harshly.

I do many animal communication readings for clients who feel guilty about their animals who have passed and wonder if they remember them fondly or are angry for the lack of attention or the timing of their departure. In the thousands of readings I have done, however, I have never had an animal complain about their experiences. They show me the positive memories, the love and attention that they received, and the fun that they had. My clients may have spent hours consumed with regret about something they feel they did or didn't do for their animal. The animal, on the other hand, has taken with them only the wonderful aspects of the way they lived and the gratitude for all that they had. Even the cat who told me that she was murdered when her human entrusted her to someone else relayed only one message back to her person: "Forgive him."

At the Gentle Barn, when we are hosting groups of people who come to us in search of hope, we take them to our wishing well and allow them to release their negative beliefs and replace them with positive affirmations: "I am lovable." "The world is safe." "I can find true love." "I am smart." "I am beautiful." "I have worth." It's not a one-time healing. It's part of a process. I still continue to release negative beliefs about myself almost every day, in addition to practicing gratitude.

Within each of us is the capability to draw on a wishing well of positive affirmations. As with meditation, it takes practice to toss the habit of negative thinking into the trash and embark on a new habit — telling ourselves that we are worthy and lovable, that there is a reason for us to be here, and that life will support our happiness if we can embrace gratitude.

Sometimes practicing gratitude can be as simple as appreciating that we are breathing. Sometimes we are grateful for the basics: a morsel of food, a sip of water, an article of clothing, a roof over our heads. Other times we are grateful for deeper gifts like a healthy body, our loved ones, and the opportunities to grow, evolve, and thrive every day.

My cows and other animals have led the way and been my greatest teachers. Through their stories I was able to unfold my own, and through their recovery I was able to become whole and full of purpose. It has been a road fraught with tears, pain, anger, confusion, self-hatred, resentment at those who hurt me, and a resistance to being here at all. With the help of the Gentle Barn cows and other animals who raised me, I saw how wonderful life can be when we love ourselves, forgive and help others, surrender to the perfect timing of life, and have gratitude for every day.

Thank you for allowing me to share the stories of my animals with you. Stories matter. Since the beginning of civilization, stories have been the way we have passed our values, insights, and other important information from one generation to the next. Often, what we hear about our place in the world when we are young is what we carry as our story. These stories can be helpful and supportive, but often the stories that we tell ourselves can be harmful.

It's both valuable and liberating to take the time to really understand the stories we tell ourselves. Does our story give us a sense of belonging, or does it make us feel separated from others? In the story we carry, do we have to live up to others' expectations, or can we pursue dreams of our own? Do we approach life with compassion and love, or do we react with fear or anger?

What stories are we telling other people? Do we fill the air with complaints, or do we communicate through appreciation and gratitude? Do we encourage the best in each other, or do we criticize first?

For two decades I have watched as the Gentle Barn cows encircled each other to celebrate birth, mourn death, meditate, and support each other. Who is in your circle? Do they support you, see you, and hold space for you in your darkest moments? What opportunities are there for us to grow stronger, find our voice, and stand in our certainty? How can we be kinder to ourselves and look at ourselves through appreciative eyes? How can we be a better version of ourselves tomorrow than we were today?

What story do we collectively tell the rest of the world? Is our story one of standing up for justice, extending help to all living creatures, honoring our bodies, and coming up with new ways to have reverence for our planet? Or is the story of our current culture one of violence, pain, greed, and destruction?

No matter what stories we were born into or accepted as our own, we all have the choice to make a change, with acceptance of the past and the courage to make the future better for all living beings.

If the planet is to thrive, if our bodies are to heal and the animals are to be loved, it is time for all of us to tell a new story. One in which lifting each other up is more important than our own success. Where empathy, gentleness, and generosity are our most treasured values. Where we embrace ourselves along with others. Where we teach our children to be proud of who they are, to protect flowers instead of pick them, to admire birds instead of chase them, to release bugs instead of kill them, and to stand up for justice toward humans and animals alike.

I hope someday you can visit one of our Gentle Barn locations. If I'm there, you'll recognize me right away. I'm the woman covered in animal hair. I smell like the barnyard and have tiny holes in most of my shirts where calves have chewed on me. Those are my lucky shirts. I have no "nice" shoes or clothes because no matter how much I intend to keep them for special occasions, I always end up wearing them in the barnyard. During the summer my house gets dusty, and on rainy days the floors in my house get muddy from the dogs going in and out. I am constantly cleaning. I often have hay in my pockets, which makes me giggle when I find it. I usually accessorize with bits of straw in my hair. And I'm the one with a content smile on my face because I love my life!

I have loved more animals than most, having been able to save and care for thousands over the years. I have said goodbye way too many times, and it never gets any easier. I have gone many times without eating or sleeping to help an animal and would do it again in a heartbeat. I would do anything I can to save a life. Being with guests in the barnyard and sharing the animals' stories fills me with a purpose like no other and makes me feel so happy that I feel like I could fly. And when I am sad, I go straight to the cows, and their embrace makes everything better.

For the first time in my life, I would not change one little thing about me or my life. I know me, love me, and accept me, and I am grateful to be living this dream and doing this work.

When you have a chance to visit us at the Gentle Barn,

please come as you are. Perhaps you're celebrating, newly in love, finding that the road ahead is full of adventure. We'd love to celebrate with you. If you're tired, ill, sad, lonely, frustrated, or feeling like life is hard, allow us to resuscitate you. Through our doors, beside our animals, you will find a moment to rest, let go, feel your place on the earth, and realign with your sense of self. There is a Gentle Barn cow who is ready to be hugged.

I'll see you there!

ACKNOWLEDGMENTS

Like all my ideas, projects, and creations, this manuscript would have never come to life without the help of the many brilliant, supportive, loving people around me. I want to thank my husband, Jay Weiner, for holding down the fort while I spent many days and late nights hidden away writing. Thank you for always believing in me and living this dream with me. I love you! Thank you, Kenneth Kales, for getting me started and listening to all my stories so patiently. Thank you, Marcia Wilke, for believing in this project, cheering me on, and helping my stories take shape. Thank you, Patricia Heinicke, for your wonderful edits. Thank you, Jason Gardner, for being my champion and guide at New World Library and bringing our animals and their wisdom to the world. Thank you, Bill Gladstone, for being my agent, bringing me to New World Library, and being the voice of reason and understanding when I felt lost. You were my rock!

Thank you to Val Smith for her beautiful drawings at the start of each chapter.

I want to thank the Gentle Barn staff, volunteers, and board of directors for working so hard and doing so much. It is an honor to work beside you. Thank you to all our donors, guests, followers, and fans, who lift us up, support us, and enable us to do this work, live this dream, save these animals, and tell their stories. Thanks to all our rescued animals who have raised me, taught me, loved me, and given me the opportunity to be the best version of myself. One day, the only thing we will do with cows is hug them; with turkeys, cuddle them; with chickens, hold them; and with pigs, give them belly rubs. And thank *you*, reader, for allowing me to share our animals' wisdom with you and for your gentle hearts that can change, evolve, and awaken to love.

ABOUT THE AUTHOR

Ellie Laks is the founder of the Gentle Barn Foundation, a national organization that rescues and rehabilitates unwanted animals and heals people with histories of trauma. She is an animal communicator, energy healer, TEDx speaker, educator, and the author of *My Gentle Barn: Creating a Sanctuary Where Animals Heal and Children Learn to Hope.*

Ellie founded the Gentle Barn in 1999 and has since hosted hundreds of thousands of people who have come there seeking hope. She is the creator of Cow Hug Therapy as well as her Gentle Healing method, which allows old, sick, injured, and terrified animals to recover using a mixture of Western medicine, holistic healing modalities, holding therapy, and lots of love.

Ellie lives at the Gentle Barn's California location with her partner, Jay Weiner, who runs the organization with her. They have three children, hundreds of animals, and much to be grateful for. Ellie wants to spend the rest of her life improving the lives of animals and opening the hearts of humanity toward them in any way she can.

GentleBarn.org • EllieLaks.com